THE DIARY OF A NAAFI GIRL

Eve Diett

Pen Press

© Eve Diett 2012

All rights reserved

No part of this publication may be reproduced, stored in a retrieval system, or transmitted in any form or by any means, without the prior permission in writing of the publisher, nor be otherwise circulated in any form of binding or cover other than that in which it is published and without a similar condition including this condition being imposed on the subsequent purchaser.

First published in Great Britain by Pen Press

All paper used in the printing of this book has been made from wood grown in managed, sustainable forests.

ISBN13: 978-1-78003-442-3

Printed and bound in the UK
Pen Press is an imprint of
Indepenpress Publishing Limited
25 Eastern Place
Brighton
BN2 1GJ

A catalogue record of this book is available from the British Library

Cover design by Jacqueline Abromeit

To my late husband Bill who played a great part in my story.

The leaves of memories unfurl at each turn of the page.

Acknowledgements

I acknowledge my friend Jacky Wagstaff who was my right hand in helping me out by typing my story. To my lovely family who believed in me and encouraged me to write the story of my life in the NAAFI. It was a wonderful feeling to go back in time and relive it all again as that young NAAFI girl.

Chapter 1

We joined the NAAFI today. Marge, my friend and I wanted to do something more exciting than the hotel job we had at the present time. So boring standing at that reception desk all day. The only bonus was being by the beach in Torquay. We had taken the hotel job for the season.

Our posting came today! We have been posted to Newton Abbot, seven miles from here. It's an Army camp, and as it is now the end of the season, our employer says that we can leave the hotel at the end of the week. Hooray!

I should explain a little about what the NAAFI is. The Navy, Army and Air Force Institutes (NAAFI) is an organisation created by the British Government in 1921 to run recreational establishments needed by the Armed Forces and to sell goods to servicemen and their families. They would run clubs, bars, shops, supermarkets, launderettes, restaurants, cafés and other facilities on most British military bases and also canteens on Royal Navy ships. This was the time of National Service, when all young men were meant to do a tour of duty in the armed forces, and the camps were always a hive of activity with recruits.

So here we are, NAAFI girls! Marge had her hair permed for the occasion, and with her fair hair looks just like "Bubbles", the NAAFI cap perches on her head like a halo!

Oh, and she even splashed out on false eyelashes! I have visions of them popping off into the tea Marge will be serving to the troops!

The overalls we have to wear are something else. Dark blue in colour – they have to be out of the Ark! Not unlike a straitjacket, they fit where they touch. To wear anything underneath but bra and pants is an impossibility and to bend is drastic as it rides up your body and ends up being a pelmet! We complained to Miss Kitty Jones, the manageress, who was very sympathetic and understood our dilemma, but explained that a new batch was on order and should be here before Christmas, but in the meantime we'd just have to grin and bear it.

Miss Kitty, as she likes to be called, is in her late forties, her greying hair scraped back into a bun. She is very tall and well upholstered in stature, rosy-cheeked and with a pleasant face.

Now, I was informed that she would like me to take control of the net bar, which is like a small self-contained shop at the end of the canteen. It stocks everything, cigarettes, Blanco, boot polish, Brasso, boot laces, toothpaste, chocolates etc. And I would be responsible for cashing-up at the end of the day with her in the office. It is rather daunting – I hope I will be able to remember all the prices.

Marge and I had a shock when we set eyes on the billet which we will share with two other girls. It's not unlike a Hillbillies shack – army surplus beds, metal locker and wardrobe. In the centre of the room to complete this picture is a combustion stove which cracks and creaks when the damper is out – it scares the hell out of me.

I met up with Marge at the Women's Land Army Rest Break House in Torquay while I was working there as an assistant to the Matron. I had previously spent two months there to recuperate from a bad bout of flu. I was a Land Girl then, but was asked by Matron if I would like to go back to help her run the place. It didn't take me long to think it over as it was a softer option than going back on the land. Marge worked in the kitchen as assistant cook and we became great friends. We were both aged 22 years and enjoying life to the full. We only stayed in one night a week and that was to get ready for the Saturday night hop at the Spa Ballroom on the front in Torquay. The cook, Maud, always gave me a quizzical look over her horn-rimmed specs and would say to me, "I think you are leading my Margie astray," and I would reply demurely, "As if I would do that, Maud!"

Just up the road was a nursing home for Airmen who had been badly injured in the War. Many were completely blind, their faces and hands badly burnt, but with all their suffering and appalling injuries they were always cheerful and never moaned. So Marge and I would call for them and take four of them to a pub called the 'Hole in the Wall' which was dark and had sawdust on the floor but was always packed to the rafters and very popular with the local seamen. There was always music, and the Airmen would take it in turns to play the piano. We never spent a penny between us but the drinks were always lined up on top of the piano. We all had a lovely time and the young men, bless them, enjoyed every minute and we staggered and sang all the way home!

Diana and Nancy who share the billet with us are like chalk and cheese. Diana is very attractive with a shock of auburn hair and a voluptuous body. Nancy is very timid with straight brown hair pushed back from her pale face with a hair grip. She's not very tall, about 5ft 2ins, and wears this shapeless overall which swamps her small body. Apparently she prefers to work in the kitchen.

The two cooks, Vera and Joan have the end room in the billet. I'm not too sure of Vera, she's very fierce and bad-tempered, so I am keeping my distance! Joan is just the opposite – lovely personality and very good-looking with short blonde hair. Apparently she is only on a short stay here, just awaiting her posting to Germany as she is engaged to an Army officer and is going out to Düsseldorf to be near him.

There are two more girls in the other billet, Elsie and Alice, who we have not yet met as they are still away on leave.

Chapter 2

Did my first stint at the net bar today. My word, it was hectic! Also daunting with all those recruits waiting to be served, pushing and shoving in what seemed like an endless queue. A very handsome orderly officer came in and sorted them out for me and said, "Welcome to the mad house! At your service any time, young lady." I went all weak at the knees and felt myself blush with a mixture of excitement and embarrassment. There was that wonderful surge of joy when his hand held mine – I hope he comes in again soon, the sooner the better!

Now, Diana is quite a character. The soldier boys and men have nicknamed her "Treacle Tart". She tantalises them by undoing her two top buttons on her overall so that a small amount of her voluptuous bosom peeps out. They shout, "Come on, Treacle, shake them boobs!" Yesterday the wolf-whistling and foot-stomping was so loud it brought Miss Kitty out of her office. To say she was angry would have been an understatement. She marched over to the Bar shouting, "What's going on out here? Diana, what are you up to?"

"Nothing, Miss Kitty," replied Diana very demurely, looking coy and quickly closing her top buttons. Miss Kitty towered over Diana staring fiercely at the young men who were grinning from ear to ear and shuffling nervously in the queue.

"Well, do you have any idea what is causing all this racket?" she asked them.

The two near the Bar murmured nervously, "We are very excited about going on weekend leave, Miss... er... er...!"

"Should I believe that now, young men?" she asked.

"Well, it's true," they replied weakly.

"In that case, Diana, get them served quickly, so they can go somewhere else to let off steam. Not, do you understand, not in my canteen," she addressed them all, "and you, Diana, I want to see you in my office later."

Yesterday Diana, little Nancy, Marge and I went into town to the cinema to see 'Gone with the Wind' starring Vivienne Leigh and Clark Gable – it was lovely. Now Clark Gable reminds me of my 'knight in shining armour', the orderly officer on the camp. I am smitten. I hope he comes in the canteen again soon!

Marge is in love! She is going out with the barber on the camp who is called Lance. He seems to be a fast worker and wants to take her home to meet his parents in Birmingham. She talks non-stop about him and is besotted.

We have been invited to the sergeants' party on Saturday in their mess. I will have to buy a new evening dress! The message received was to be prepared to do the sword dance! The sergeants are from a Scottish regiment, so perhaps a kilt would be more suitable than a dress. No way could I imagine myself in a kilt. But Diana said that she would, just for a laugh – never a dull moment here!

My day off and I'm going into Newton Abbot to buy my dress for the party! I am still on the lookout for my 'knight'. Marge said he is most likely married or otherwise engaged. What a depressing thought.

Miss Kitty left me a note for me to see her when I returned this evening, wonder what that is all about? Have not been here long and she has offered me a promotion and training to be an assistant manageress. What a surprise, I was not expecting that so quickly. I hope I am able to match her expectations of me. She has given me six days to think it over.

Managed today to purchase a lovely cocktail dress in black lace with a pink taffeta lining, it was in a sale. Also, I had enough money left for a pair of black suede court shoes. I must have a dress rehearsal later – I wish the party was in the officers' mess then perhaps I would meet my orderly officer and our eyes would meet across a crowded room! I can just dream.

We have a new batch of national service lads on the camp, quite a few of the others have been drafted out to another army base. Before they left they were so excited about going, thinking that they were going out to fight, because they had this vision like a boy's own story adventure, a wild sort of carnival crusade. The newspaper at this time does not help, with snappy pictures of young recruits smiling and waving when boarding the train and saying goodbye to their loved ones. But on the other hand they would have been sent out to that bloody hell-hole battle in Korea and some may never return. And to me they were all heroes, especially when they came in to say goodbye to me and the other girls in the canteen in their shiny new uniform caps, smiling and eager to go into action.

Elsie and Alice are returning next week, which is good news, for we are short staffed. Big attraction in the kitchen today, we have a new male chef who was posted from Germany. There is a buzz all around with the staff. But why, I wonder? Anybody would think he is the only male around but there are thousands out there on the camp. I shall have the pleasure of meeting him later on – it's a joke!

I met him and he's quite a ladies' man. He is tall, about 6 foot with blond hair, probably from a bottle – well, he has dark roots so it could be! I suppose in a way he is quite handsome in a rugged fashion but with one great big ego. He fancies himself something rotten and is forever posing and preening when he thinks we are not paying him enough attention. The cooks think he is god's gift. His name, by the way, is Vincent but he prefers to be called Vinnie. He asked me if I would accompany him for a walk round the camp to get his bearings and I replied that I would give it some thought.

I learned later from Diana that he had asked all the girls, "So join the queue, Eve," she said.

Today I encountered a chap called Zig the spiv! He is new to the camp but has set up quite an enterprise, so I understand. He has a good thing going flogging watches, irons, cigarette lighters, even booze etc. When he came into the canteen, I was asked by him if I needed a new watch – 9 carat gold, and he would do me a deal. I told him I was not interested but he kept on insisting – he was annoying me no end. I just had to get firm and tell him in no uncertain terms to get lost and move away from the Bar, so I could get the rest of the boys served. The queue was stretching out across the canteen by now. I expect he had fleeced the boys of their wages. Oh and by the way, his mate is called Slippery Sam – I wonder where he got that name!

Zig is typical of many in the camps who dealt on the black market. They popped up at various places and were mostly on national service and out to make some money out of the unfortunate ones who had spent their money on gambling, playing cards or in the local pubs.

Today I met Miss Kitty's boyfriend very unexpectedly. This could prove interesting! They were having a kiss and cuddle in the store cupboard! I think he was getting quite hot under the collar, as his face was puce. I was so embarrassed, I felt such a fool and kept saying, "I'm so sorry, so sorry."

Apparently he is the sergeant major on the camp. I kept wondering what the hell he was doing in the cupboard – strange place to have a love tryst! But then again why should I be surprised at anything that goes on around here. And lo and behold, I walked out of there without the stock that I had gone in there for in the first place! He was a short little man and she was tall and heavily built and he looked as though she could have picked him up and put him in her pocket. What an odd couple!! It takes all sorts!

We had our dress rehearsal in the billet today and we paraded up and down in our finery. Margie looked great in her little black number and gold high heels. Diana – well what can I say? She went well over the top with a flared pleated skirt and a tight-fitting top in bright red, with a plunging neckline and covered in sequins. To complete the ensemble she wore red high-heel patent shoes. I was under the impression it was going to be one of those nights!

Today I met Alice and Elsie. Alice is very tall and slender with short blonde hair and she is engaged to a corporal on the camp called Archie. Elsie is quite a contrast, 5ft 2ins in height, quite stocky and plain and she has an almighty chip on her shoulder. She informed me that she is the chargehand in the canteen, and is going to make some changes about the place. "When?" I asked.

"I have her wrapped around my little finger which you will all soon find out," she replied haughtily and tossed her head. My, my, I thought, there is trouble ahead. I expect there is going to be one heck of a power struggle! I refrained from mentioning my offer from Miss Kitty of training to be assistant manageress. I will shelve that one for a later date, after we see how the land lies.

Marge and I are going onto town this afternoon to the dress and fashion store where we bought our evening wear. While we were there at that time, the manager of the store asked us both if we would like to come in and model cocktail dresses and evening gowns. He went on to say that it would be ten sessions and he would pay us well, so we consented at once to his generous offer. We explained to him that we could only do this when we were off duty and he was quite happy about this. So here we are branching out as part-time models. Margie is so excited, she thinks she might be 'discovered'. I am more concerned about my savings account looking healthier.

Zig the spiv was in again today. Miss Kitty threatened to report him to the sergeant major. But I doubt that very much, as she bought two watches from him yesterday, and one was a gold-plated gents' watch. Now guess who is going to be receiving that as a Christmas present?

Ding, dong in the kitchen. Pots flying in all directions! Reason, the ovens were not heating up. I volunteered the suggestion that it may be the way the wind was blowing and was met by an icy stare and a sarcastic remark from 'wonder boy', something along the lines of, "F…, f…… weather cock are you now?" Ah well, just another day at the ranch! No doubt little Nancy will get the blame for not cleaning out the flues properly.

Diana informed me that 'wonder boy' was looking for me and that he was slumming it in the NAAFI with the lower ranks. She said that she rather fancied him herself, and that if I was not interested in him, she would certainly make a play. That remark rather spoiled my romantic dream of my 'knight'. There are no secrets in this place – perhaps he will ring me later, at least he sounds interested.

It was a great party at the sergeants' mess – in fact it was hilarious. Diana was so funny, especially when we did the sword dance. Hopping in and out on those crossed swords was some feat, but Diana's dance was more like a hornpipe. She got completely carried away then tripped up and ended up legs akimbo with her short skirt fanning out to reveal bright red frilly knickers!

"Which cracker did you acquire them from, Treacle?" enquired one of the sergeants – where the hell did she get them from?

"Well, girls," Diana replied, "let's see what big mouth has got on under his kilt!"

We dragged her out before all hell broke loose, with the sergeants shouting, "Don't go now, girls, not now the party is just getting exciting!"

We held her in a tight grip knowing full well that if we let her go she would be back in there like a shot, with all the whiskey she had been drinking. Diana was tanked up to the eyeballs, and we knew that Diana always took everything to the extreme. Miss Kitty remarked, "That girl will get herself into serious trouble one of these days, but I will make sure that it isn't here."

The sun is shining and I feel it is going to be a lovely day. I am off duty meeting my 'knight' outside camp. He rang me last night and his name is Robert. We are going to Torquay for lunch then on to the theatre in the evening. I can't make up my mind what to wear – I have had three dress rehearsals already!

There is a lot of activity going on around the camp. I think they may be getting around to some big occasion. There are more parades than usual and everything getting painted white. Even the kerb stones around the huts and the dustbins are getting a coat of paint. I think if anyone stood still long enough they would get painted too!

Robert was a great guy, a perfect gent. We spent a lovely day in Torquay. We walked along the beach and later had lunch in 'Bobbies' on the front. I knew the owner of the restaurant from my days working in the hotel. So we were made very welcome and given VIP treatment. When it came to paying the bill the waiter said, "Boss says it's on the house."

Before going on to the theatre we indulged in a cream tea at a little café, with a lovely view of Torbay. It was a lovely day and I did not want it to end. When Robert kissed me goodnight at the Barrack gate he said, "Let's meet up again next week on your day off."

I walked through the camp on cloud nine only to be met by Nancy wailing, "I can't stand it here anymore!"

Needless to say I was brought down to earth with a bang. The tears were running down her face and she blubbered, "Oh, the bastards made me scrub the bleedin' floor on me hands and knees," and through intermittent sobs added, "and all the greasy pans."

She threw herself on her bed howling, using her sheet to mop up her nose which was streaming. I managed, after a while to calm her down and made her a cup of tea and sat with her until Margie and Diana returned from duty. Then, with a much calmer Nancy went with her to try to sort out this problem with Miss Kitty.

"Well, Nancy, what is all this about?" asked Miss Kitty. Nancy tugged nervously at her overall skirt and just stared at the floor.

"Come on, Nancy, tell me who in the kitchen has upset you."

"All of them," she replied, "I can't stand it any longer. I want to leave."

"Now come on, Nancy."

"But I can't help it," sobbed Nancy.

"Now, now, my dear," said Miss Kitty putting an arm around her shoulders, "Now leave it to me. I will sort things out in the kitchen and also make sure you have more help. Now, run along with Eve and off to bed with you and no more crying."

Today everything is quiet on the kitchen front. Nancy is happier and wonders will never cease, Vinnie is helping her with the pots and pans. When walking through I noticed I did not have to duck to avoid flying missiles!

The Army chaplain paid us a visit this afternoon. He was quite at home with his feet under the kitchen table and the cooks fussing over him, being fed buttered scones just out of the oven. The table was laid out like a banquet – cakes of all descriptions. Diana and Margie were taking advantage of this special treat and smiled at the padre. He was a small fair man with a pair of steel-rimmed specs perched at the end of his little turned-up nose.

"I was wondering, young ladies," he said, peering at us over the top of his specs, "if you would like to join the Women's Guild in the village. It would be an exceedingly good gesture, after all it would pave the way to good relations with the locals. The parish vicar says that you would be very welcome."

Diana stood up and smiled at the padre, "Now that is most kind of you. Would you like some more tea, vicar?"

Naughtily, Diana leaned over him with the teapot. The poor man was beside himself as she was showing quite a low cleavage and a close view of the top half of her ample bosom. His hand shook, his cup clattered precariously against the saucer and the tea was slopping against the sides as he brushed through the roots of his thinning hair. He pushed back his chair and with his hand still trembling, he put the cup down and stuttered, "I have an important meeting er… must go er…!" and with great difficulty he made his escape through the canteen door, missed one of the steps and almost fell into the arms of the sergeant major who remarked jovially, "Must take more water with it, padre!"

Chapter 3

On arriving on duty this morning we were met with utter chaos. The canteen storeroom had been turned over by thieves and they had stolen the entire cigarette stock. The office door was lying on the floor and the safe, we noticed, was not there anymore. How on earth they managed to cart that away amazes me, for I think it must weigh a ton. Military police are crawling all over the place, so at present the canteen is closed to the troops.

We have been given the task of cleaning up the mess they left behind. One thing to be thankful for, Miss Kitty and I had banked the bulk of the cash the day before.

We are opening up tomorrow. The military cops found the safe underneath the canteen, (the huts are mostly on stilts) and guess what, unopened! They had tried out various implements in a bid to open it up, but to no avail. Battered but still intact, it is now back in the office.

Today the canteen was packed to the rafters with troops and I did not have time to talk to any of them, which I usually do when there is a lull in the queue. Many of them think I am their agony aunt. Most of them are very young and have never been away from home like this before, and thrown in at the deep end. They realise it's not so glamorous, this army life hey are living it, with the constant drill by the sergeant shouting at them and the name-calling.

One lad came in last week with a 'Dear John' letter. His girlfriend had run off with his best mate and through his tears he sobbed, "I trusted him to take care of her while I was away." So I did my best to give him my words of wisdom, that his mate had probably done him a great favour and that a girl like that was not worthy of his love, and as the saying goes, 'there are plenty more fish in the sea'.

He asked, "Do you think I should write to them?"

"Well, put it this way," I replied, "Just write to your mate and say, 'Good luck, I'm having a whale of a time here and there are many beautiful girls here on camp. I am just off to a dance with one of them' and then sign off − 'it was nice knowing you'." Then, days later he came into the canteen with a bunch of roses and a card saying, 'to a lovely lady'. I was so pleased to think that my advice had helped him to handle his problem and that there is a wonderful life at the end of the tunnel for him, I hope with a lovely girl.

Today one of Miss Kitty's married daughters came for tea. She was a replica of her mother, a stout overpowering girl. I was asked by Miss Kitty if I would bring into the office a pot of tea, scones and some of cooks' delicious Eccles cakes. When I went in with the tray, they were discussing some rather absorbing medical details. I wanted to know more in case Miss Kitty was suffering from some ailment. I dreaded to think if she was and I would be landed with taking over from her. So, I loitered outside the door and listened!

"Oh dear, she's forgotten the blasted sugar," spouted Miss Kitty, "go into the kitchen for me, Poppy dear, and then you can report back to me what that lot are up to."

"Oh Ma, do I have to?"

"Yes, you do," she said, "they are having the life of Riley lately. The cook is an imbecile and not worth the wages she is paid."

I was furious but made a quick exit into the kitchen before 'Poppy dear' came out, grabbed the sugar bowl and returned with it, very haughtily and slammed the bowl down on the tray and said, "I do hope you enjoy your scones and Eccles cake that our very good and hardworking cook baked specially for you!"

'Poppy dear' looked at me with her mouth open, and Miss Kitty asked, "Is everything alright with you, Eve? Oh, and by the way, my dear, do thank cook for me. She is quite a treasure and I don't know what I would do without her! Oh, and before you go, Eve, how's it going out in the kitchen?"

"Fantastic," I replied, "We are all working flat out and I think everyone is due a break. So would it be alright if we all stop for a cup of tea and an Eccles cake?"

She replied, "Oh, most certainly, go into the canteen and take half an hour!"

How dare she slag Joan off. She is a damned good worker and a lovely lady and an excellent cook. I think I will have to be on my guard in future and not take people at face value. Why, oh why some people are so two-faced is beyond me. That's my moan over for now!

Vinnie was in a bad mood today, grumbling at everyone in the kitchen. I happened to drop a metal tray, by accident, on to the floor behind him.

"For god's sake," he wailed, "watch what you're doing. My head's splitting!"

"I am so sorry," I replied, "very thoughtless of me."

Diana chimed in, "He had a very rough night out on the tiles!"

Vinnie retorted, "Go and jump in the f...... river!"

Joan made him a cup of tea with a splash of whiskey in it. "Now get that down you, a hair of the dog is what will cure you, you misery!"

The weekend was rather a strain on my nerves. I had to cope with an over amorous M.P. who followed me everywhere, even into the stock room where I was trying to do the stocktaking. He was a pest, asking me when was my day off and what time did I finish at night.

"Please, go away, I am busy. And to answer your question, I have a boyfriend."

Cheekily he said, "But I won't tell him and we can have fun and make hay while the sun shines. Come on, be a sport!" Thank god Miss Kitty came in and he stopped in his tracks.

"What are you doing, Sergeant?" she asked, "harassing this young lady. Haven't you got better things to do? Come on now, out of my stock room, can't you see we are very busy after the break-in?"

He replied cheekily, "But I could stay and help." To which she retorted, "Oh, no you don't. Out, now OUT!"

"Oh well, be like that!" he said, and to me, "See you later on, Miss."

"Are you going out with him, Eve?" Miss Kitty asked.

"No I am not, and he's been pestering me most of the afternoon." I retorted. "I was so pleased to see you walk in, he really scares me!"

"Well, don't worry, Eve, I'll see that he doesn't come into the canteen while we are working," she said, "Leave it to me, and I'll send Diana in to help."

Oh no, I thought, not her!

We managed to get through the stocktaking. Diana was on her best behaviour, but on the odd occasion was hanging her head outside the window, puffing away on a ciggie! I had forbidden her to smoke in the store room just in case she set light to something – she was that madcap!

So to say my nerves were a jangle was an understatement. I was sorely tempted to partake in a nip of brandy. I sometimes wonder what the hell I am doing here!

This morning I received one hell of a fright! I was just about to put the floats out for the Bars, when pulling up the metal shutters, this large Alsatian dog charged across the canteen and made a beeline for me, snarling and baring its teeth. It put its large paws up on the Bar, its lips receding to show these massive gnashers. I gasped with fright and bolted back into the kitchen, dropping the cash, which rolled around the floor in all directions. I shook like a leaf and shut the kitchen door with a bang.

"Hi, Eve, what the hell is going on?" Miss Kitty asked, dashing out of the office.

I replied breathlessly, "I think one of the camp guard dogs has escaped. It's… it's out there now." With that she ran out to the Bar and Joan, the cook and I listened at the door. Miss Kitty was giving someone a piece of her mind in no uncertain terms.

"Get your bloody arse out of my canteen, you evil bastard. I will report you to your commanding officer; and take that bloody animal with you. Don't you dare harass my staff again, we have a job to do here and the safety of my staff is paramount. Have you got that?" she asked angrily. "You are a pillock, first class to boot!"

"Well done," we chorused, "Miss Kitty, you were amazing, you certainly told him where to get off!"

"He won't be bothering any one of you again, believe me. Now, come on girls, get this show on the road," she retorted, "and by the way Eve, grab that broom back there and go and sweep up the float money."

Marge, on coming in asked, "What's going on?"

"Nothing to worry your head about," said Miss Kitty, "You just get that tray of buns and cakes out on the Bar and check the tea urns."

"So come on," she addressed us all, "jump to it, let's get the show going. The time's getting on and the soldier lads will be queuing up and biting at the bit to get fed and watered."

My, she was one gutsy lady and her vocabulary was great, especially the French!

Chapter 4

ENSA, the entertainments committee on camp have arranged for a Hypnotist to come and entertain us. They are holding the show in the main Hall. His name is 'Marcel the Great' and he's had very good reviews. His last show was at the Winter Gardens in Torquay, so he must be good to be accepted there. I must arrange time off, we all want to go. So Marge and I are going to ask Miss Kitty this afternoon; fingers crossed she'll say "yes".

We can't believe our luck, we have all been given the time off! Miss Kitty reckons that all the soldier boys will be at the show, so she didn't think it would be worth opening up at that time, but would open for an hour after the show.

"So mind, I want you back here then. No skiving off, especially you, Diana. No funny ideas of going off with your boyfriend until you have done your stint on the Bar."

Several of the girls want help in giving up smoking, so they are keen to volunteer to be hypnotised. Well, that is going to be a tall order! Alice chain-smokes, so I don't hold out any hope for her, but if he is as good as they say, well miracles do happen. So it should be a night of surprises. Margie's wish is to have more confidence; mine is to challenge this 'Marcel' in a battle of wills. I might live to regret that statement! Diana said she will bet me a pound that I would go out like a light, to which I replied, "You wish!"

This afternoon I have a date with Robert, he said he wanted to give his old banger of a car a run out. Well, well, surprise, surprise – no way was it an old banger! When I met him outside camp, he was sitting there, smug, grinning from ear to ear in a spanking new red sports car.

"Come, Evie," he said, "jump in, we're off on a mystery tour. Don't look so worried, sit back, relax and enjoy the ride," he chuckled. The blasted seat was so low it was with the greatest difficulty that I had to keep my tight skirt from riding up.

"God, Evie, you are a fidget, what's up?" he asked. Bloody hell, I thought, my blasted skirt – I wish now that I had worn a dress.

"Nothing," I lied. "Well, to be honest there is, Robert," I said, "what time will we be back as I am on duty at 6.30?"

"Oh, for heaven's sake don't worry, I'll get you back on time. Forget that place. We're going on a jolly," he said, "it's a lovely day. Do let us enjoy these fleeting moments away from the rat race on that camp."

It was a lovely day, apart from the skirt which had a mind of its own. We ended up in Brixham, had a ride in a speedboat across to Torquay and visited Kent's Cavern in the docks. That was lovely with the stalactites hanging gracefully down from the ceiling of the cave in amazing colours, and the lime deposit stalagmites coming up from the ground in spires. Whilst there we had a Devon cream tea, then back to the quay to get the ferry back to Brixham.

It was one of those days when you did not want it to end. It was fleeting moments of joy. My, he is so handsome – guess I am smitten!

Today Robert went away to Scotland, on a course for six long weeks. Marge said, "Think of it making the heart grow fonder!" I hope.

Next week I am on ten days' leave and I'm going home to Worcester – I can't wait!

When we entered the hall it was packed to the rafters with the troops and the only seats vacant were in the front row. 'Marcel' was on stage, viewing his audience. He was a tall, gaunt-looking man with close-cut black hair smoothed back with Brylcreem. He was wearing very tight black, satin trousers that did not leave much to the imagination, a bright red silk or satin shirt and a green waistcoat. He strutted around the stage like a peacock. Wolf whistles were going around the room and a shuffling of feet.

"All right now," says the sergeant major, "settle down now, lads. Come on now let's give Marcel our support, after all he has come here to entertain us." There was loud applause; the room seemed to be charged with excitable energy.

"Now then," says Marcel, "let's have some volunteers," looking directly at us all sitting in the front row. Diana rose to her feet.

"Ha, we have a lovely young lady. Come this way, dear, don't be shy," he said in a sugary voice and helped her up on to the stage. "Well, young lady," he said, "is there anything you'd like to ask me before you sit down?"

"I can't think of a thing," said Diana, very demurely.

"Well, have you a special dream or wish that you want to achieve?"

Diana looked up at him, fluttering her false eyelashes, "Well, Marcel, I have often dreamt of being a ballerina," she said.

We all gasped in astonishment, titters went round the room and some wag at the back shouted, "Good on yer, Treacle!"

Marcel's reply was, "I may be able to grant your wish, go and sit over there." Now looking over at us he said, "Let's have all you young ladies up here." Oh hell, I thought, I was hoping I could somehow get out of it.

The young lad who was sitting by me at the end of the row said, "I'm game!"

"But, but he said young ladies," I replied.

He winked at me, "Hell, that doesn't matter, let's go up, it'll be a laugh."

We steered him to the front, "And lo and behold we have a brave young soldier," Marcel gushed, "Now what's your name?"

"Charles," he replied.

"Well, Charlie boy, what can I do for you?"

"I would like to be cured from smoking because my girlfriend and I want to get married, but I seem unable to save very much."

"Right, Charlie boy, go and sit over there. I will cure you," he said.

I whispered to Alice, "You go next," and to Alice he said, "Are all you beautiful young ladies in the ATS?"

"No," replied Alice, "we're NAAFI girls."

"Well, my lovely, what's your name?"

"My name is Alice," she replied.

"And what is your wish?" he asked.

"I would like to be cured of smoking."

"I will certainly do that for you, go and sit over there by Diana."

I was next. "Well now, brown eyes, what is your name?"

"Eve," I replied.

Jokingly he said, "Is there an Adam out there?"

"No there is not!" I replied.

"Well, go and sit at the back of the stage," he said.

I was a bit peeved that he had not asked me my wish. He strutted to the back where I was sitting and his weak watery blue eyes looked down on me; he smiled and I noticed his rotten teeth. I felt at that moment like a victim.

"Look into my eyes," he commanded. Instead I concentrated on his bulbous nose.

"You are now feeling sleepy," he chanted on, "you are now going into a deep deep sleep, and when I count to three you will awake."

"I am not asleep," I said, "in fact I am wide awake!"

He leant over me and muttered through the side of his thin lips, "Sod off the stage!"

To excuse my sudden departure he addressed the audience, "One young lady changed her mind, well you can't win them all; now let's have two more brave soldiers and then we can get on with the show!"

Diana was first on his list. She went out like a light, so did Alice, Joan and Charles. Then there were the three other volunteers, one sergeant and two cooks, Dan and Alf who were quite characters. They often came into the canteen and always full of fun. So it was quite interesting to watch their antics.

Marcel spoke, "Now Diana, your wish has been granted. Your name now is Charmain, you are a famous ballerina and you will address the audience and say, 'Ladies and Gentlemen, my name is Charmain and now I am going to perform Swan Lake for you,' and when I click my fingers you will rise from your chair and dance."

When she spoke to the audience it was with a strong, clear voice; in fact it was very refined and we looked at one another in complete surprise.

The soldiers clapped and cried out, "Come on, Treacle, give us a pirouette!"

Marcel gave them all a black look and tossed his head in contempt.

In fact, Diana did exceedingly well. She danced around the stage, then did a curtsey and skipped back to her chair. Her head slumped down on to her chest and Marcel clicked his fingers three times and said to her, "You will awake now and go back to your seat in the audience."

There was uproar from the troops, clapping and stamping of feet, "Good on yer, Treacle!" they shouted.

Diana looked at me bewildered, "What's all that about?" she asked. She had no recollection of her debut on stage at all. To me, that's scary!

Alice was next. She had told Marcel that her wish was to quit smoking for good.

"One, two, three you are now in a deep, deep sleep," he said, "and will awake when I click my fingers three times. From now on Alice, you will not ever smoke again." He then proceeded to lift her gently on to the backs of two chairs, then chanted over her, "Deep, deep sleep."

He then moved away one chair from under her and then the other, and there was Alice, as stiff as a board, with no support at all, just floating there! He then put his hand in the small of her back and gently pushed up and she floated there in mid-air. He then brought her back down on to the backs of the chairs.

Believe me, it was spellbinding. There was complete silence in the hall; you could have heard a pin drop. I just could not comprehend how she floated there like a feather – absolutely amazing!

He eventually awoke Alice and she came back in to the audience, but on doing so he asked her to go into the third row and sit next to the handsome young man and politely ask him to move up one seat so that she could sit at the end of the row. Then to say to him, 'please may I have a cigarette?' you will take two puffs, then spit it out because it tastes so horrible. And, sure enough, she did!

We had to leave before the show ended to open up the canteen. Alice was very subdued, which to me was unusual and she left early to go back to the billet. Miss Kitty sent Diana over to make sure she was alright and remarked darkly, "No good comes of anyone messing around with your head, it's not natural!"

Diana came back saying that she was snoring away, so we breathed a sigh of relief.

The boys were full of their experience with 'Marcel' and were convinced it was, "pure magic!" What I saw back there with Alice certainly gave me food for thought; I'm not sure how the hell he did that, for there was nothing underneath her when she floated in mid-air, and there was me thinking it would be quite a normal day today!

After the excitement of last night Marge and I had planned to go to the cinema, as we were both off duty at the same time which hardly ever happened. As we all trooped up to the canteen Miss Kitty met us in the kitchen and asked, "Where's Alice?" We all said that we hadn't seen her.

"Eve, go back to the billet and get her," she said angrily, "I'm not having her skiving off – tell her to get up here right away."

I found Alice snoring her head off. First I shouted, "Come on, Alice!" but to no avail. I tried shaking her, but still no response even after I had sprinkled cold water on her face. She definitely was out for the count! I was just about to report back when Miss Kitty came into the room.

"Well, why is she not up and dressed?" she asked angrily.

"She is in a deep sleep and I cannot wake her," I replied.

"Out of my way," she retorted, "I'll get her up. Come on, Alice," she shouted and lifted her into a sitting position. But still Alice snored on.

"Ring the MO Eve, right away and get him over here at once. I think that hypnotist has messed with her head!"

The Medical Officer was not best pleased at Miss Kitty's request and demanded angrily, "Is it an emergency?" Yes, I replied and went on to explain Alice's problem.

"I'll be over right away," he said. Subsequently he also failed to arouse Alice and suggested we went in search of Marcel, to come back and bring her out of the trance. He said, "I understand he is putting on a show in Torquay, so I should head there right away before he moves on." He arranged for Army transport with a driver, and I was asked by Miss Kitty to go.

Margie said, "I'll come with you."

"Well Marge, are you on duty today?" asked Miss Kitty.

"No," was Margie's reply, "it's my day off."

"Just checking, in case anyone else has any ideas of jumping on the bandwagon!" she said.

Alas! We had a wasted journey in Torquay for Marcel had moved on to Exeter. We tracked him down eventually in Exeter but he was not very keen on coming back to camp. When we approached him he was just getting ready to have his afternoon siesta so was not in a very pleasant mood. He stamped his feet and looked at me fiercely as if to say, how dare you upset my routine! So, I was thankful we had Nick, the MO's driver with us who said in a very calm manner, "I have orders from the Commanding Officer that you come back at once to work your expertise on the young lady, who is in a deep sleep and we are unable to wake her so we need your help. After all you were the one who put her in this state when you hypnotised her at the camp last night."

Very reluctantly he came with us muttering, "This has never happened to me before…"

"Well," I replied, "there is always a first time!" He just gave me a withering look.

Marge dug me in the ribs and whispered, "Just ignore him!" He was so blasted arrogant – what an ego!

Miss Kitty welcomed us back with relief. We were hoping to get a cup of tea but she hit that one on the head with, "Well done girls, now go and hold the fort while I take over here."

Marge and I did manage to partake in a cup of tea and Joan the cook said that we could help ourselves to fresh scones straight from the oven. Alice came bouncing into the kitchen followed by Marcel and Miss Kitty.

"Well done, Alice," we said, "how do you feel?"

"On top of the world," was her reply, "never felt better, but I'm starving, will it be alright if I help myself?"

"Go ahead," said Miss Kitty, "but I have a much better idea." Looking over at Marcel, who was standing there preening she asked, "Would you honour us, Marcel, by staying to tea?"

With a toss of his head and a slight wiggle of his body he replied, "Champion! I will be delighted."

Looking over at me she said, "If you would be so kind and bring in a pot of tea and cakes and scones. Oh, and butter them, and we will take our tea in the office." I felt like saying, "Right, Captain!" I feel that at times she looks on me as her personal maid! Margie was hiding behind Joan, and giving the salute! Alice had the impression she was invited too, so she dutifully followed in their wake; Miss Kitty looked back at Alice, "Not you, dear," she said sweetly, "go and join the rest in the kitchen!"

It is unprintable to write what Alice's comment was when the door shut behind them!! So, here goes, another day in the life of a NAAFI girl!

Chapter 5

The 'psycho' military policeman seems to have gone to ground. I have not seen hide nor hair of him since the incident in the canteen. But, I still have that uneasy feeling that he is just awaiting the opportunity to get me when I am alone; I just can't shake that feeling off. Marge reckons I have a vivid imagination and that he is just a bully. I mentioned it to Miss Kitty and she said, "I can assure you, he would not dare to harass you again, but just make sure that when you go out of camp to go with one of the girls."

Well, they are all on duty, and as it's my day off I just want to go into town to buy a new coat. I was often told by my mother, to take a hat pin or a box of pepper if I felt unsafe. I think I'll pass on the hat pin and take a box of pepper. Goodness knows where you would stick the hat pin – my thoughts raced along to a place where the eyes would water!

I caught the Army base bus outside camp. There were quite a number of the new recruits on the bus going into town, it was quite an experience! Rick Potter was the driver and the lads told me that they had named the bus, 'the bone-rattler'. I could not have named it better myself, for if you had anything loose it would have fallen off!

Rick was a fiery redhead, his face full of freckles – a real 'cheeky chappie' with his army haircut standing to attention in spikes so that he found it difficult to keep his cap on. So he threw it on to the dashboard muttering, "Bloody thing!" He called out, "Bums on seats. Hang in there, Streak Lightning at your service!" We took off like a bat out of hell – he certainly lived up to his nickname. He puffed away on a Woodbine cig which sent out this spray of sparks, and some wag at the back of the bus shouted out, "Watch what you're doing, Streak, you'll set your 'tache on fire and make a bonfire!"

He retorted, "Shut yer cake'ole mate, or I'll come and stick one up yer hooter!" He drove like a maniac down those winding country roads and I prayed that no other vehicle came in our direction or else I could see us taking a detour across the fields! One poor cyclist ended up in the hedge and Streak wound down the window and shouted at him, "You silly sod, you should look where you're going!" He then laughed out loud and said, "Ha, well he's moving – he ain't dead!" He looked over at me, "Are you enjoying the ride, Miss?" – I did not utter a word! The seats were wooden so you just slid from one side to the other when he took the bends. I was thankful I was sitting alone, for if anyone else had been there I most probably would have ended up on their lap – not a good way to get acquainted! Also, it was the slamming of brakes that put the fear of god up me, I was sure the bus was on its last legs!

At last we reached our destination. I stopped and asked Rick the Streak, what time the bus returned to camp. He replied, "On the hour, outside the Station. Where's the boyfriend? I expect the sports car is much more comfy than this old jalopy!" I was taken aback, seems there are no secrets on camp! No reply from me.

"Many thanks, Rick. Enjoy your day," I said with a smile. After that hair-raising episode, I made my way to the nearest café for a much needed coffee to steady my jangled nerves, although really a brandy would have been better! I planned not to hang around the shops for too long as I had to get back to the camp in the daylight. It was getting quite cold and later on it forecast a frost.

I managed to buy a lightweight sheepskin coat. Diana said that she was going to creep into my room in the night and put it on to sleep in, for it was icy cold in their room and the bloody army blankets were threadbare – they must have been around in the Great War! It has taken me months to save up for that coat. The shops are still not very well stocked and many items are scarce as we are still recovering from the War years.

We had our first flurry of snow yesterday but it did not lay. Vinnie informed us that it would be two feet deep by the weekend, so there would be "no gallivanting to town for you girls! And when the wind whips up over those fields the narrow roads will be impassable."

"Well," I replied, "there are snowploughs."

He laughed, "How would you like to make a bet on that?"

"I am just going to be optimistic," I said.

"Please yourself," he remarked, "but I hope you've brought your wellies!"

To be on the safe side, after Vinnie's descriptive weather forecast, we are going into town to buy boots this afternoon. Diana moaned, "I've been saving up to buy this smashing dress and now it's a toss-up – boots or dress?"

We all chorused, "Boots, because Di, you would not get very far in your high heels!"

Vinnie retorted, "You'll most likely break your bloody neck. Ha, ha, ha!" Diana was just about to clock him one with a pan when we grabbed her and took her firmly out of the kitchen.

Good news, I received a letter today from Robert. He hopes to return to camp this weekend and says his life is empty without me. Suddenly, my life is full of sunshine! I may get to ride again in 'Red Jet' – that is the name he has given to his car. But if so, no tight skirt this time. For it sure had a mind of its own – I go hot and cold at the memory of it!

Marge said, "You worry too much, I'm sure Robert didn't mind!"

"That's the point," I replied, "I don't want to give him the wrong idea."

Marge replied, "My motto is, if you've got it, flaunt it!"

Alice is quite full of energy since her long sleep, and still no temptation to smoke again. When I remarked on how well she looked, she said that if the occasion arose again to be hypnotised, she would go for it!

"Well Alice," I replied, "make sure it isn't here as I don't fancy driving round the countryside looking for any more 'Marcels'."

We are at the weekend now and no snow, but freezing cold and frosty. The hedgerows look pretty though, with silver cobwebs looking like lace, and with the pale winter sunshine they sparkle like gems. Last night the wind whistled around the billet. We stoked up the combustion stove to keep the place warm through the night, but that was a mistake as the noise it made kept us awake all night! It was so blasted noisy, it roared away like some demented animal. I had visions of us all taking off into the night with it, the cold air freezing that ancient contraption – it is not getting stoked up tonight! Diana will moan but she can sleep through anything. Marge and my beds are right opposite the monster, and even the corrugated roof creaks and cracks from the heat of it, especially when it's in full throttle! So, we have decided to raid the cupboards for extra blankets.

Nancy gets right under her blankets, just the top of her head is visible. It's a wonder she doesn't suffocate! Little Nancy always looks so sad, we always try to cheer her up and invite her to come out with us but she always says that her brother wants her to go home in her spare time. She only lives ten miles from the camp and her parents are both dead so the brother likes her to go home and cook for him. Diana says to tell him to go and get lost – the lazy sod!

The parade ground is like a sheet of ice. Perhaps, today the troops will have a day off but Margie said, "I expect they will be ordered out there to clear it!" Well anyway, it would at present make a very good skating rink.

I was thinking, when those metal shutters go up in the canteen, it reminds me of a stage and all the recruits are actors. Full of character and from every walk of life, every day is a different experience. I weave stories in my head of the various ones that have passed through here. I love the crazy ones who make us laugh and the mimics taking off the sergeant major. The very young ones who have never been away from home before, shyly trying out their chat-up lines on us girls. We always let them down gently and make time to chat to them when we can. Then there are the 'spivs' with their sales repartee and the talented ones – the pianists who tickle the ivories on the old piano in the canteen, making various types of music and not forgetting the artists who bring their drawings and paintings to show me.

It is so nice to have Robert back here on camp again, but sadly not for long. He is returning to Scotland in four days and he thinks that he will be posted from there to Singapore in the very near future. My day off tomorrow and Robert is taking me into town. I have to be outside camp at 10.30 in the morning. I have had two dress rehearsals already – not sure what to wear, but tight skirt is definitely out! I still go hot and cold at the thought of it. I sometimes wish I could be like Diana, who doesn't give a damn about anybody or anything!

We have a new girl coming from the village to help out. She starts next Monday. There seems to have been an influx of troops and we are rushed off our feet. Alice is on leave for seven days. I received a card from her yesterday saying that we would all be surprised when she tells us her good news. I can't for the life of me think what that could be! When I was reading the card out in the kitchen to the girls, Vinnie said, "I bet I know what it is!"

"Go on, enlighten us," retorted Diana.

"Can't you guess?" he asked.

"No, we can't," we all chorused.

"Well," he sniggered, "I expect she's up the duff!"

"You evil perisher!" Diana said angrily, "trust you with your one-track mind!" and with that she lobbed a cabbage at him which was on a side table waiting to be chopped up. Vinnie ducked and it ended up with a great splash into a pot full of tomato soup. It erupted with great force and splashed everywhere, even up the walls. We all made a quick exit from the kitchen, leaving Vinnie with his mouth wide open with his hands on his head!

Outside we all fell into a heap, laughing. Marge remarked, "That sure was one hell of a bullseye!"

My day off and a date with Robert when we have planned to go into town. There was me, thinking we were going in his sports car, but what a surprise, Robert was waiting for me outside the camp and said, "I've decided to give the old banger a rest, come on Evie, let's board the old Rattler into town."

Nick Potter was grinning from ear to ear winking at me wickedly and said, "Welcome aboard for the mystery tour!"

"What's he hinting at?" asked Robert quizzically.

"Beats me," I shrugged my shoulders, "he's just being flippant."

"Bums on seats," shouted Nick, "Streak Lightning at your service!! No bad language at the back there, you squaddies, we have an officer and his young lady on board today so keep it down!" he said.

It was a freezing cold day with lots of ice patches on the roads. I wore my new sheepskin jacket and felt the bee's knees in it. Robert said that I looked very elegant and was pleased to walk beside me. *That* made me feel on cloud nine! Nick Potter drove very gingerly into town – no hair-raising episodes, and I did notice he was wearing his cap, even though it was balancing at a jaunty angle on top of his spiky hair. What a character! His parting words were, "Don't do anything I wouldn't do!"

We went to the Copper Kettle for a coffee, then went shopping. Many of the shops were already displaying Christmas gifts and Robert asked me to help him buy a birthday present for his mum. And I bought, with his help, a pre-Christmas gift for my brother Jim, an Airfix kit of a Lancaster bomber, which I know he will be pleased with. I will soon have to make my Christmas list. We had a 'Ploughmans' lunch in a pub and then went to the cinema which was featuring a film with Fred Astaire and Ginger Roberts. Before the film we were entertained by 'Charlie West on the Organ'. It arose from the floor at the front of the stage and was all lit up in various colours which flashed around the cinema. He played all the popular songs and asked everyone to join in and sing as the words appeared on the screen. It was great! We ate a large box of Black Magic chocolates and Robert kept pinching all the hard centres.

Fred and Ginger danced beautifully; that Fred Astaire certainly had magic feet – it was lovely. I had seen the film before, during the war, but it was just as good the second time around. On coming out of the cinema Robert said that he fancied fish and chips. So we queued up at the chippy and sat on this grotty bench in a bus shelter and ate them, and both said how good they tasted. We were so busy talking that by the time we walked back to the station to catch the Rattler back to camp we had missed it. So we hired a taxi back, and Robert said what a lovely day we had had "and we will have to do it again, my love."

When he kissed me goodnight at the barrack gates he said that he would see me again in two days' time, but it would be in the evening when I came off duty. Just when I was about to walk away towards the billet he called, "Evie, come back."

"Yes Robert, what is it?" I asked.

"I have this small gift for you," he said.

"Oh Robert, thank you," I replied.

"Open it up when you get in," he said. As I slipped it into my pocket my mind was racing. It was a small box; I felt all around – could it be? No, can't be, not a ring at this stage, he would have said something. My thoughts were going into overdrive; I don't know a lot about him, really. He never talks a lot about his family, and I haven't a clue where he lives. It's just like I have been swept along with the moment!

On entering the billet, the girls were all sitting around the stove, drinking cocoa.

"Well," they said, "come on, get a chair and give us the low-down on your day off with 'Prince Charming'."

"I'll be back in a second," I said.

"Don't be long," they shouted back, "we're dying to know."

I made my way to the sanctuary of the bathroom to open my present. I was all of a whirl – what could it be? After dispensing with the gold paper and ribbon, I lifted the lid and there nestling on the blue velvet was a dainty pair of horseshoe-shaped gold earrings encrusted with small sparkling stones. Before putting them back in the box, I tried them on and they were beautiful.

Looking in the mirror, when I turned my head from side to side they held this brilliance when the light caught them. My, I thought, could they be diamonds? I quickly put them back in the box and into my handbag and decided not to tell the girls of Robert's gift. For, to me, it was too precious to share!

Chapter 6

Another hectic day in the canteen; Vinnie is not speaking to any of us, sulking about the episode of the cabbage and the soup. Ruby, the new girl, came today to help out in the canteen and kitchen. Joan and Vera both said that it's about time we had more help. She's a pretty girl with jet black hair which cascades around her shoulders, with deep blue eyes and a jolly personality – a trim little figure. Vinnie perked up no end! He said to her, "Don't let that lot lead you astray." As if we would!

Yesterday Ruby went on the bar for the first time. The poor girl had one hell of a chaotic time; the troops all flocked to her bar demanding, pushing and shoving and asking to be served. Ruby was in a real state! I overheard one soldier bragging that he had three packs of ciggies free and was going back for more. That angered me, so I slammed down the shutter on the net bar and went over to help her out.

Ruby was near to tears, "I am so scared," she said, "There are so many of them and I can't remember all the prices!"

"Don't worry," I said, "leave it to me." In a firm loud voice I said to them, "Now all of you form a queue, single file, no messing about or I will shut the bar down. Do you all understand?" There was silence, and by magic half of the queue disappeared out of the canteen. They, most likely, were the ones hoping to get freebies! One wag called out, "Right'ho Sarge!" I surprised myself, where did that authority come from?

"Well done," remarked Miss Kitty, "you handled that well. I can see I will have no worries when I go on leave."

I replied, "I'm not quite that ready." She just smiled.

It was a great surprise to us all to see Ruby turn up for duty today; we all thought that yesterday's fiasco would have scared her off. Miss Kitty asked Diana to help her out for a while, until she gets the hang of it.

Today Alice returned from her leave, so we were all awaiting to hear her news. We all sat on Alice's bed, and she told us that Archie had proposed and they were getting married two weeks before Christmas and it will take place in Torquay. Apparently, Archie has been promoted to sergeant and is being posted to Germany in January, which is why they didn't want to wait. When Archie is settled out there he will send for her!

"That calls for a celebration!" we all chorused.

"With what?" Diana asked.

"We have a choice," I said, "lemonade, cocoa, Horlicks or coffee, take your pick!" They all chimed, "Coffee." Elsie moaned, "I don't like coffee, it keeps me awake."

"Well, Elsie, what will it be?" I asked.

"I think I'll have cocoa," she replied.

"Alright then, Elsie," I said, "it was very kind of you to help me so you run along and put the kettle on and I will get the cups out." Diana looked over at me in surprise, for Elsie was always very prickly and never put herself out for anyone.

When we were in the kitchen looking around for the tin of biscuits to go with our coffee Elsie asked, "Why is Alice going out to Germany?"

"To be with Archie," I answered.

"But it's a long way," she replied.

"What's that got to do with it?" I said, "they are in love and that's all that matters. And one day when you fall in love. Elsie, I'm sure you will feel the same."

"No hope of that!" was her reply.

"You will meet someone one day," I said, "and you will fall head over heels, you wait and see." And she actually smiled at me – now that's a first! Poor Elsie, she wants to lighten up a bit and find out that life is not too bad after all. I would like to help her, but in this place I do not even have enough time to do all the things I want to do.

We awoke this morning to snow; there was a blizzard of snowflakes swirling around. The troops were busy clearing the parade ground and pathways to the cookhouse and canteen. It is so cold in the billet it was a relief to go over to the kitchen to warm up. Joan had the large ovens heated up ready to bake the pies and cakes. Vinnie was moaning that he was freezing cold last night and couldn't sleep and had to get up to put on his overcoat. He was warming his back against the ovens and Joan said to him, "For goodness sake, Vinnie, shift your backside so that I can get the pies out. You wouldn't make a good soldier!"

"Well in case you hadn't noticed I am a chef," retorted Vinnie.

"You could have fooled me!" Diana remarked.

"Trust you to put your two ha'pence in," said Vinnie.

"Well look at you, standing there moaning and heating up your backside while Joan does all the work!"

At that moment Miss Kitty came in, just in time before all hell broke loose. "I need you, Vinnie," she said, "in the stock room, to check all the produce we will want to be in stock before this weather gets worse." He followed her like a little lamb!

Yesterday, Ruby was still having a problem with serving on the bar even though she was getting plenty of help from us all, and I decided it was just not fair to her to put her through what she obviously saw as an ordeal. I had a word with Miss Kitty and she proposed that she should help Joan and Vera in the kitchen.

Today it is still snowing, but no blizzard. We have a huge snowman by the side of the billet built by several of the young lads. It has a carrot for a nose, chips of coal for eyes; they've even adorned his head with an army cap and a khaki scarf round his neck – it is a work of art! The only problem is that every time I come out of the billet it scares the hell out of me as I forget it's there, and when I see it I think it's that creep the military policeman! I haven't seen him around for a while, with his ferocious dog, so let's hope he got Miss Kitty's message loud and clear.

Chapter 7

The roads are quite clear at the present time, so we are still able to make it into town. Diana and I have both started Christmas present shopping and we are also going to start collecting for a wedding present for Alice and Archie. Joan and Vinnie are making the wedding cake. Marge says we must hurry up and start collecting early while everyone still has money in their pockets, as the nearer it gets to Christmas the less people will have and we'll end up with a pittance in the collection.

Last night Miss Kitty invited me to go with her to see the ballet 'Swan Lake' in Exeter.

"But," I asked, "who is going to hold the fort while we have the night off?"

"I have that all arranged, Joan is going to take over. She is more than capable," she replied and continued, "It was no use asking Henry," (he's the boyfriend from the cupboard) "when I mentioned I was thinking of going he said, count me out, the very thought of men prancing around in tights leaves me cold!" So I have a date with Miss Kitty on Saturday night – oh, and we are going in her ancient Austin 7. I hope to god I don't have to crank it up!

This morning Diana gave me an unexpected bear-hug. When I got my breath back I asked, "What's that in aid of?"

She replied, jumping up and down, "I'm in love, mad, crazy love!"

"Well, Diana, when you come down off cloud nine, tell me who this 'Prince Charming' is."

"First of all," she said, "promise me you won't laugh when I tell you."

"Me, laugh?" I replied, "as if I would, Diana. Is he one of the soldiers on the camp, do I know him?"

"No you do not," she replied, "He's not in the Army, he is – wait for it, and don't you dare laugh – a farmer!"

To say the least, I was lost for words.

"Well, Evie say something," she implored.

"Sorry Diana, I was just having this vision of you milking a cow! Where the hell did you meet him?" I asked.

"On his farm, well not entirely his farm, he works with his dad," she replied. "It was like this," she went on, "I decided to go into town on my day off but was too late to catch the Army bus, so decided to walk into the next village and catch the local bus from there. But I got lost, went down the wrong lane and ended up in this farmyard; and there before me was a sight to behold!"

Oh god, I thought, this story is getting more and more intriguing and bizarre.

I chuckled, "What did you see, a vision?"

"You promised you wouldn't laugh."

"I am sorry Diana, go on," I said.

"Sitting on this tractor was the most gorgeous hunk of a man; it was love at first sight. His name is Roger Dodge!"

"I can't help it, Diana!" I curled up laughing, "Roger the Dodger!" She chased me all round the room throwing pillows at me until one burst open and all the feathers came cascading out, like a snowstorm! At that precise moment Marge came in followed by Elsie. Marge got covered in feathers but she laughed, "What, for goodness sake is going on?"

Elsie stormed off covered in feathers too, shouting, "Grow up, act your age!"

We all burst out laughing. We were there till midday clearing up the feathers before going on duty. We had the brilliant idea of opening the window and throwing them outside onto the snow but it was one of those ideas that do not work to plan. For alas, they kept blowing back in again! Diana says she will tell me more about Roger later – I can't wait!

It is much warmer in the billet, most likely because we are surrounded by snow which has drifted to form a bank against the wooden walls. The camp looks picturesque with the snow-capped roofs of the billets, it is not unlike a Swiss canton, but alas no tinkling of cow bells or yodelling, just the occasional roar of the sergeant major drilling the troops. We decided to name our snowman, Fred.

We have a young lad helping out in the canteen and kitchen, his name is Charles. He has been given the jobs of clearing the snow outside the canteen and spud-bashing in the kitchen for the cooks. Poor Charles is on 'jankers' for dropping his rifle on parade. He fares quite well in the kitchen, with Joan and Vera feeding him up on buttered scones and cakes. He was only there until midday then went over to the main cookhouse spud-bashing.

Diana remarked, "It's just as well we don't have anything like that in the NAAFI or I would be on permanent 'jankers'."

Vinnie piped up, "More like the glasshouse for you!"

"Shut your cakehole!" she retorted.

"What's a glasshouse?" asked Ruby, "is it something like a greenhouse?"

"Forget it," Diana replied, "I'll draw you a picture later." Poor Ruby always manages to come in at the end of a conversation and never gets the full story. Then, from out of the blue she blurted out to Diana, "I saw you coming out of Dodges farm on a tractor with Roger!" Vinnie's ears pricked up, and in all innocence Ruby went on, "Was he giving you a ride?"

It went deathly quiet, Diana was mortified and blushed to the roots of her hair. Vinnie jumped in smirking and said, "Rube, tell us more!"

With that, Diana fled from the kitchen. We asked him why he was so nasty to Diana and he answered, "I don't mean it, it's just a bit of fun."

"Well," we all said, "it has got to stop."

"Let's put it this way," I continued, "harmless banter in the workplace is alright but when it gets personal and also affects your private life then that is not acceptable."

"Oh you girls, you always take things so seriously," he said.

"Well, we are on your case. So watch it!" we chorused.

It was the last thing Diana wanted for Vinnie to find out about her boyfriend Roger, but then in this place one cannot keep any secrets. We suggested she invited him to tea. "I think that will stop the tongues wagging," I told her.

We managed to collect enough money to buy Alice and Archie a canteen of cutlery for their wedding present. Marge has told Lance to get lost! The reason is that he was getting too possessive and she felt suffocated. It is Robert's last weekend before he goes back to Scotland, so we have a date on Sunday and I've managed to get the evening off. Miss Kitty wasn't very pleased because Henry had planned to take her for a spin in the Austin 7 – can't wait to get behind the wheel. He does not know what awaits him – especially in this weather!!

Today we had a delivery of Christmas goodies in for the net bar; Christmas cards, boxes of chocolates with decorative pictures of winter scenes and various other pictures of sweet little kittens and snowmen. Not unlike our Fred but without the hat and each box decorated with ribbon. It is so nice to see things coming back to normal after the war. It was a pleasure to dress my shelves in the net bar in a presentable manner with the goodies; we have all been rationed for so long during the war. I remember one time waiting in this long queue outside a sweet shop to buy six chocolates, and when I eventually arrived at the counter they had sold out. And I had wanted them so much for my young brother James for his birthday.

What a relief! We did not go in the Austin 7 to Exeter to the ballet owing to the freezing conditions. Miss Kitty's boyfriend Henry (sergeant major) had arranged for us to be given a lift into Exeter in an army lorry. The driver, Dusty, was going there to pick up rations. We sat up in the front of the cab.

Climbing up into the cab was hilarious, being that it was so high up. I sprang up with such force that I nearly ended up in Dusty's lap. He chuckled, "Cor blimey, I thought my luck was in!" Miss Kitty was having difficulties so she asked Henry to give her a bunk up. He pushed and shoved, then she managed to get onto the seat.

"Oh hell," she said, "I think I have split me drawers!" We roared with laughter – Miss Kitty away from the canteen was a different character with a wicked sense of humour.

We enjoyed a lovely night out. Henry had thought of everything. There he was outside, waiting for us in a jeep after the show had finished. Goodness knows where he got that from! He wrapped army blankets around us both, "Can't have you lovely ladies getting cold!" he said. He proceeded to delve around in his inside tunic pocket and brought out a flask, "Now come on, my lovelies, take a swig it will warm you up!" he said. It was brandy; I thought the fumes alone would have kept us warm!

Miss Kitty said to him, "Henry darling, where did you get this fire water from?"

He replied, "From my Yankee friend Elma, Kit my love!"

We arrived back at camp all aglow which was just as well because little Nancy had let the stove go out and it was freezing in the billet.

Diana was full of mischief today. On her way up to the canteen this morning, she broke off one of the largest icicles which was hanging from the roof of the billet. She voiced that one of her intentions was to put it down Vinnie's back when he was bending down to open the ovens, or the other crazy idea was to put it down his trousers! We all chorused, "Please don't, Diana, he could very likely get burnt – it's crazy and it's dangerous."

"Oh, trust you lot, it would have been a bit of fun!" she retorted. Instead she held the icicle behind her back, then addressing Vinnie she said, "Close your eyes, I have something for you. Hold your hands out."

Vinnie was taken aback. "Stop messing about" he said.

"Oh well in that case if you don't want it I'll give it to someone else," replied Diana.

"Oh go on then, you minx, here goes – my eyes are shut," and with that he put out his hands and Diana put the icicle into his outstretched hands.

Vinnie shouted out, "You b… bitch!" and proceeded to chase her round the kitchen with the icicle, threatening to put it down her back! Good job Miss Kitty had the day off!

Joan quickly came in to dampen Vinnie's rampage. She shouted, "Vinnie, your cakes are burning! The smoke is coming out of the oven!" That stopped him in his tracks, shouting to Diana, "I'll catch you later, you can be sure of that!" Diana laughed, "Not if I see you first!"

For the rest of the day I kept Diana close to me. I even had her helping me in the office – cashing-up, which did not go down very well with Elsie who moaned, "I should be doing that, not her." On the other hand I could not think of a better solution to keeping the peace and the place running smoothly.

It is still freezing cold and the arctic wind sure as hell whips up over those vast fields. Fred the snowman is now a block of frozen snow with an icicle hanging from his carrot nose; Margie says it looks like a dewdrop!

A new batch of troops came in today so I had one long queue on my bar, all buying their Blanco, Brasso, shoe polish etc. for their kit – it was hectic. There are not many boxes of the Christmas chocolates left so we have had to order more.

Robert and I went to Torquay. We were invited by Josh, a great friend of his, for dinner at the hotel that he owns. We spent a lovely time there. Josh asked Robert, "Are you and Eve an 'item'? Are you serious?"

There was silence and I felt my face flush. Then Robert said, looking at me smiling, "Well, it's early days isn't it, Evie?"

"Yes," I replied, "very early days!"

"How do you cope with him always going away on his travels?" Josh asked. I replied, "Well, that's my life, here today – gone tomorrow."

Robert leaned over and held my hands in his, "Oh, that sounded so sad, Evie, I'll be back. How could I not, I would be a fool not to, you are so lovely."

"Here, here!" said Josh.

But when we kissed goodnight back at camp, I had that uncanny feeling that it was goodbye. I cannot explain it at all.

Margie reassured me when I told her saying, "It's the way you are feeling at the moment, a bit down owing to the sudden departure again. You will soon be back on form again. You are blessed with that inner strength – we all believe in you. So you, of all people, are not allowed to crack up and that's an order!"

Nancy is away on leave so Ruby has taken over the filthy job of cleaning out the flues of the ovens. Poor Ruby, it's a thankless task, for if she doesn't get all the soot out the fires do not burn well, then the ovens don't heat up to the cooks' satisfaction and then the cooks vent their anger. Also there is the lugging in of buckets of coal into the kitchen. Ruby was so distressed this morning she was in tears, running down her face in black rivulets, so Marge and I helped her out. We fastened scarves round our heads and put on some very old overalls. Well, I should say I wore the only scarf and Margie had an old tea towel round hers. We made coffee for Ruby and told her to sit down while we got on with the job. We soon discovered what a manual job it was and soon started to regret my kind offer of taking out the big pan of soot. The blasted stuff had a mind of its own and showered me from head to foot. Marge was outside filling the buckets with coal. Then I heard this almighty crash; I stopped what I was doing and opened the door to see what it was.

There was Marge lying flat out in the snow and ice with the empty buckets and coal everywhere! Marge sat up laughing, I said, "It's not funny, what are you laughing at?"

"It's you," she said, "I can just about see the whites of your eyes, you look just like the golliwog on the marmalade jars!"

"Oh come on, get up for god's sake, Margi, and let's get these bloody fires going before the cooks and the rest of the girls come on duty," I said crossly.

"Oh how your eyes sparkle when you're angry!" was her answer.

"Right Margi, now you can get the rest of the soot out and I'll get the coal in."

Soon we had the fires roaring away. Then I went volunteering again saying, "Pass that pan of soot and I'll take it out to the bin," which went well until I tried to descend the steps without spilling any, then to my horror just as I was about to empty it into a large bin, a gust of wind came from nowhere and soot flew into the air, all over Fred, who was now black and white, and Marge and Ruby were sprayed with the rest. That is definitely the end of my volunteering!

A sleepy Diana met us in the billet corridor heading towards the bathroom. She burst out laughing, "Bloody hell, for one moment I thought the Arabs had invaded!"

This evening we have all been invited to a pre-Christmas social at the sergeants' mess. The cooks have been putting the finishing touches to the food for the buffet and we have been searching through our meagre wardrobes for something to wear. This will not take me long as I only have my cocktail dress in black and pink lace. Alice is borrowing my long dirndl skirt and white Hungarian blouse which is hand-embroidered with red roses around the neckline and puffed sleeves. Diana said, "I wanted to borrow that."

"Well, for one thing," Margie said, "the skirt would swamp you, after all Eve is five foot six and you are a 'short-arse'! I would say you are about five foot two."

Diana replied, "Big head, I meant the blouse!" Margie burst out laughing, "You wouldn't manage to get one boob in never mind two!" Needless to say Marge made a quick exit before the missiles flew through the air, and I followed her.

It is still freezing cold and we have great difficulty keeping the billet warm. Alice, Marge and I are suffering from chilblains; mine are on my feet which are agony when they get warm. Ruby passed on to us her granny's cure.

"First one is, walk in the snow in bare feet. Second, if that doesn't work, wait for it – put your feet in the pee pot!!" Personally I will stick to my own remedy, Snowfire cream and invest in a pair of woolly bedsocks. The very thought of putting my bare feet in a pot full of piddle fills me with horror. Alice asked Ruby, "Have you tried it?"

"Not at all," replied Ruby, "I don't get chilblains but my granny does!"

I have a new admirer; his name is Richard and I met him at the sergeants' social. We danced the night away. He is a good dancer, brilliant at the Tango and we won first prize! Richard's prize was a leather wallet and a bottle of champagne, mine was a silver powder compact and a box of Black Magic chocolates tied with a red ribbon. At the end of the evening he shared the champagne with us all. Diana was in her element all evening. It was hilarious when she did the jitterbug with this very stocky sergeant. He was swinging her in all directions, through his legs, over his shoulders; Marge said, "Let's hope she's not wearing those red frilly knickers!"

Diana should have won first prize if only for the sheer entertainment. She is a minx but we all love her, she is so full of fun and energy. I can't for the life of me see her as a farmer's wife, but she has told me that she is head over heels in love with Roger and he feels the same. Marge and I have been invited to the farm on Sunday to dinner. Roger is going to pick us up in his dad's car. Diana said, "Don't you two let me down. I want your support as he is going to introduce me to his mum and dad."

I said, "Don't worry, Diana, just be yourself and they will love you."

Marge murmured, "Whatever did you tell her that for!"

This afternoon I went with Alice to Torquay. She was hoping to buy a pair of white satin slipper shoes to go with her wedding dress. But we hunted high and low to no avail, so she said that we'll give Newton Abbott shops a go at the weekend. I think I have now qualified to draw a map of all the shoe shops in Torquay!

Today we finally found a perfect pair of white satin slipper shoes, and, to our surprise, it was the first shop that we went into. So Alice is happy and so am I, because I don't think I could have faced any more shoe shops! I even had a nightmare about shoes, but we won't go into that! So on a lighter note, I did manage to buy myself a lovely suit. I am so thrilled with it! There it was on the mannequin in the fashion shop window and I was drawn to it like magic.

I said to Alice, "I have just got to have it!"

She replied, "But it might not fit."

"It has just got to," I said.

I approached the assistant and asked her if it would be possible for me to try on the suit that was in the window. She looked me up and down and replied, "It looks to me as if it will be a perfect fit. It's a Susan Small suit, the jacket is fully lined and it's in our sale."

Alice nudged me saying, "Go on, ask her the price, you may not be able to afford it." But that fell on deaf ears as I was determined to have it, regardless. It fitted like a dream and I paraded up and down for their approval. The lady assistant put her hands together and clapped, "Perfect, perfect!" she purred, "Will you be taking it, Miss?"

Alice nudging me again whispering, "Go on ask?"

"How much is it?" I asked.

"Three pounds ten shillings," was the assistant's reply. I only had two pounds three shillings in my purse, so I asked if I could put a deposit on it. She replied that she would have to ask the manageress, just wait here.

Alice delved into her handbag and produced one pound seven shillings, "Here, take this, you can pay me back when we get paid next week."

"But you will need that money, Alice, every penny," I said.

"Here, take it," she said pressing it into my hand, "If I run short Archie will lend me some money," she replied.

It is silver grey with powder blue trimmings in the 'New Look' style, with long pleated skirt that reaches just above my ankles and the jacket is nipped in at the waist with frilly pleats at the back, not unlike a small bustle. I am on cloud nine!

"I am dead jealous!" said Marge, throwing a pillow at me when I was parading up and down the billet.

"You look so grand!" remarked Diana.

Marge asked Alice, did they have any more like that in the shop?

Diana piped up, "Come off it, Marge, if they did it wouldn't suit a short arse like you!" With that Marge threw a shoe at Diana just as 'woe is me' Vera came in the door and the shoe just whistled over her head and hit the wall behind Diana.

"Why I bother to come in here to see you mad lot is beyond me, you are all crazy!" Looking over at me and looking me up and down, standing with her hands on her hips and sneering, she asked, "What fancy dress are you going to?" then turned on her heel and out of the door, shouting as she went, "I am going to report you mad lot!"

Diana laughed and said, "I am going to put a sign on our door saying, 'You enter here at your peril. Danger is the name. Danger is the game!!'"

Well, just another day in the life of a NAAFI girl!

Chapter 8

This morning I went to the Post Office on camp to get stamps and change for the floats. On the way back I was taken unawares by this bounding Alsatian dog heading straight towards me. By luck I was not very far from the telephone kiosk so ran like hell towards it. I just managed, by the skin of my teeth to get there and slam the door behind me, as I could feel his hot breath on my heels! And there it sat, outside the kiosk snarling at me and every time I ventured towards the door it gave out a massive growl! It must be the 'Psycho's' dog, I thought, god, I thought he had left the camp as Miss Kitty had reported him last time. I waited and waited for the blasted animal to move off and time was ticking away. So being as I didn't have any money with me I decided that this was an emergency and delved into the bag of change so that I could phone the canteen.

Miss Kitty answered, "Where the hell are you? We're waiting to open up and we can't do that without the money for the floats, so I suggest you get back here pronto!"

"But, Miss Kitty, I can't. I am holed up here in the telephone kiosk and I dare not open the door because outside is that ferocious brute of a dog and I'm sure it's the same one that jumped the counter in the canteen!"

"If it is that evil b...... again I'll have his guts for garters! Hang in there while I get help."

In the meantime I was on the lookout for whoever was coming to rescue me when I saw in the distance a ground-floor window, of the brick-built barracks of the military police, open half way up. Then I heard a shrill whistle, the dog pricked up his ears and bounded off towards the window. While I watched in amazement the dog sped up and just jumped through the open window. Then it closed after him! Was I relieved to escape from my temporary freezing prison! All this aggravation just because I refused his advances: now that is scary – it unnerves me no end!

Striding towards me was the orderly corporal to escort me back to the canteen. I was so relieved to see him as I was still shaken up by the ordeal, and my feet were so cold I think they had given up the ghost on me. It took me a good half hour to thaw out when I got back.

The gallant corporal who was called Marty said to me, "My, that manageress of yours is one feisty old bird! The last I saw of her she was marching forth to see the commanding officer. I wouldn't like to be on the receiving end of her tongue! But then, she is one hell of a woman – ideal to have on your side when there's trouble around. Salt of the earth I would say!"

We heard on the grapevine that the 'Psycho' had been posted overseas; "Best place for him," remarked Miss Kitty, "good riddance!"

I gave a sigh of relief at this news, I will not have to worry anymore; I was never ever quite sure if he was watching me, waiting for the opportunity to pounce. While I was trapped in that kiosk I prayed that someone would walk by or come to use the phone, but alas not a soul – the camp was unusually quiet that day.

Yesterday we went to dinner at Roger's farm. Diana, Margie and I were picked up by Roger in his dad's old Bentley. That engine purred along those lanes. The interior of the car was immaculate, plush leather seats, excellent leg room and gold woven cords to hang on to.

Diana was very nervous, unusually quiet and she hung on to my arm whispering, "Don't you dare stray far from me when we get there!"

I whispered back, "Roger will look after you."

There was no need for Diana to worry about meeting Roger's parents. They were lovely and hugged and kissed her saying, "We welcome you into our family. You make our lad very happy!"

We tucked into roast beef, roast potatoes, Yorkshire pudding, and apple tart and fresh cream from their dairy.

"My, that was scrumptious! Our cooks feed us well but that was more like home cooking that my mum makes." Diana had dressed down for the occasion and was not her normal bubbly self. She hardly spoke a word at the table and I caught her eye at times and she looked at me as if to say, let's get out of here! Later, I remarked to Margie about it and she replied, "Where did that lovely, funny Diana go? That romance will not last!"

I have just about bought all my Christmas presents, so when I get a spare five minutes I will wrap them. My bank balance has gone down alarmingly so Margie and I are going in to Newton Abbot to the fashion store to see if they have any more modelling jobs for us to do.

It's only a few more days to Alice's wedding and we have all got time off for the event. When I say all I mean Diana, Margi, Joan and me; the others are holding the fort. Alice and Archie are going to London for their honeymoon. Archie is being posted to Germany in January but Alice is going out to join him in February so we will have her for a few more weeks.

There is an army corporal called Ray who constantly stands at my bar. I don't have much time to talk to him because of the endless queues, but he mentioned to Diana that he was going to buy me a Christmas present. Oh no, I thought, how am I going to handle this one? I don't want to hurt his feelings, so tomorrow if he is still there I will make time to talk to him. There is no way I want him to buy me any present as I do not wish to be obligated to him in any way. Diana said to tell him to push off but I couldn't do that.

Vinnie is away on leave so it's all rather quiet in the kitchen.

Surprise, surprise I have received a letter from Robert. He is coming to stay at the camp for the weekend and says he has something to tell me. Now that sounds ominous!

Last night Diana went to town with Roger. She fell into our room, through the window, at 2.15 this morning, giggling and with such a clatter that Margie threw a shoe at her! Goodness knows what she had been drinking but she was as high as a kite – perhaps the rough cider at the farm!!

This morning the young recruits, whom I had got to know quite well, came to say goodbye. They were going on a consignment to that hell hole of a place, Korea. One young lad, Ken, broke down and cried, the tears running down the dear lad's face. Through his tears he said, "I don't want to go, Eve."

I hugged him and tried to reassure him that it would not be as bad as he thought and he asked me to write to his mum. I felt so helpless – politicians have a lot to answer for. After they had all gone I went over to the billet and wept for those dear lads and sent up a silent prayer, 'oh dear God, why? Watch over them and keep them safe.' We see them all when they come in here, looking so out of place and vulnerable, it's maybe their first time away from home – they are so young and inexperienced of life in general. Miss Kitty gets cross with me and tells me to toughen up and let things go over my head and says that we have a duty to do here and we are no good to anyone if we take it all personally.

"So, cheer up and keep smiling. Remember that one day you will take over as captain of this ship when I go on leave!" Not yet, I hope!

Alice's wedding day and we have all been up since the crack of dawn, getting spruced up for the occasion. It was manic, everyone wanting to get into the bathroom at the same time. I played it crafty and arose early and was first; they were all running around like headless chickens and Diana couldn't find her stockings and was having a hissy fit! 'Woe-is-me Vera' was moaning because we had woken her up and kept muttering, "You are all mad!"

Margie said that her new court shoes pinched so I suggested putting some vinegar-soaked paper in them to soften the leather, "Trust you to come up with something like that! I would smell like a fish and chip shop and wouldn't that be nice wafting around the church!"

"Well in that case, Marge, you'll have to wear your other shoes!" I said as I hurried out of the door and left them to it, before they started hurling missiles at me. And there was me just trying to be helpful! The snow is still lying around and it is very cold but there is pale watery sunshine and a reddish sky, so it looks like being a lovely day. Fred the snowman is now one block of icy snow and some wag has put a bow tie on him and a bright red carnation buttonhole. We are all going to the church in Rick Potter's bus, the bone-shaker, so that should be fun!

Alice looked amazing! Diana had put Alice's hair up and it just hung in ringlets. Miss Kitty gave her a diamanté silver comb to put in the back of her hair and she looked so elegant. I noticed Miss Kitty wiping away a tear from her eye and she said to us all, to have a lovely time, and then went over and gave Alice a hug. Rick had decorated the front of the 'bone-rattler' with ribbon which draped over the bonnet and he sported a peaked cap which sat jauntily on his spiked hair. When boarding the bus he gave us all army blankets and said cheekily, "Keep all you lovely ladies' legs warm!"

"Bless your cotton socks, Ricky," said Diana, "but what is that peeking out of your tunic pocket?"

He replied, "That's my flask of spirit to keep me warm, but don't you worry, I'll not be sipping it while I'm driving! I've promised Archie to get the Bride Alice and all you lot safely to the church on time and it's more than my life's worth not to do just that or the Sarge will have my guts for garters!"

The wedding was one of those lovely days to remember. Alice was a beautiful bride, so graceful, she looked a picture in her wedding gown; and there was Archie looking so proud and smart in his Army uniform. The brass buttons on his tunic shone like gold. After the service we all trooped outside the church for the photo session, to be met by a flurry of snow. It swirled around us all lifting Alice's veil in the air. It certainly was a white wedding. Rick showered us all with two boxes of confetti, so what with the snow we all ended up with it sticking in lumps to our clothes. On the ride back to camp on the army bus we sang many songs including 'Roll out the barrel' and tried to remove as much of the confetti from our clothes as possible. Diana said she would have to get rid of hers later as it had travelled too far down her cleavage, which brought laughter and offers of assistance from the recruits at the back of the bus!

Miss Kitty, Joan and the rest of the staff had done Alice and Archie proud with a great reception in the canteen which they had decorated with Christmas decorations while we were at the wedding. They had all worked so hard and Vinnie, with Joan's help, had made the cake. It was three tiers and the icing decoration was splendid with pink and yellow roses. Alice wiped a tear from her eye when she saw it in all its splendour on the top table – they had certainly kept that surprise well hidden!

Several of the recruits had tied old army boots and tin cans to the back of Archie's old Morris car. One of the lads told me that Zig the spiv had put a smoked kipper up the exhaust pipe. I do hope not, I retorted, but he nodded his head and said that he had. In that case they were sure as hell going to smell that before going on their journey; I was in a dilemma, should I tell Archie what I had heard? When I told Miss Kitty she said to leave well alone, he is most probably not telling the truth – you don't know these squaddies like I do! Oh, I forgot to mention that I caught the bouquet when it was thrown by Alice and I thought, well I haven't met him yet! But Margie said, "You're next, Eve!"

Alice and Archie are on their honeymoon in London now and having a whale of a time visiting the galleries and theatres. I received a card today and no mention of the kipper, so Zig was shooting a line after all!

Robert called for me yesterday and we went to the village pub, 'The Horse & Wagon' for lunch. Then, lo and behold he confessed that he had been/was engaged to a girl named Amy. Then the 'heartfelt story' went like this, "First of all, my love, I do care for you very dearly."

Oh yeah, I thought, so here comes the dreaded 'but'.

"But, the chains of my family are too strong for me to break. I am truly sorry that I have not been honest with you. You see, the two families have been great friends for years and well, we are devout Catholics, and it's just expected of me." Oh god, I thought, how long is this going on for? If he soon doesn't end it I sure as hell am going to tip my bowl of soup over his arrogant, pious head!

At last I said, "Stop there, I get the message loud and clear."

His last words were, "My love, I wish things could have been different. Please, let's still be friends!"

I pushed my chair back angrily and retorted, "What makes you think for one moment that I would want to be friends with you? Why lead me on? I would have admired you more if you had been honest in the first place. Friends indeed, just don't flatter yourself, goodbye Robert!" and with my head held high I walked out of the pub, leaving him with his mouth wide open and a look of shock on his face. The old locals chuckled away; it had livened up the pub – a bit of drama! Perhaps, I thought, I should have done the 'grand finale' and tipped my bowl of soup over his head! It amazes me, what world does he live in – 'Friends,' indeed!!!

That is one of my New Year resolutions, not to get too close to any man again until I'm sure. Men!!!

Life goes on, Christmas next week and I am going home after all as Miss Kitty says she wants to stay on camp. I am pleased about that.

Chapter 9

Zig the spiv came in today, told me he was being posted to Singapore in the New Year. I asked, "Are you looking forward to it?"

His reply was, "You bet. It will be a piece of cake – who knows, I may return a rich man!"

"Good luck to you then," I replied.

"My mate 'Slippery' is taking over from me," he said.

"We'll miss you, Zig," I said.

"I'll miss you too, Evie, especially the way your face lights up when you smile!"

To my surprise he pulled out from his tunic pocket a pair of nylon stockings, "There you are, Evie, a Chrissie present from me!"

I uttered my thanks but said, "I can't accept them."

"For goodness sake, why not? They're kosher – I paid for them with my hard-earned pay!" Then grinning from ear to ear his parting words were, "Merry Christmas and Happy New Year!" then cheekily saluted me and walked out of the canteen door leaving the nylons on the bar. They were so fine, Dupont 15 denier – what a lovely gift, an unexpected one from Zig, of all people. The fellow does have a heart after all! The best Christmas present of all as they are like gold dust and so expensive to buy.

My new admirer, Roy came into the canteen today carrying a large flat box in gold and silver with a large red ribbon bow. Placing it on the bar he said, "For you, Evie, as I promised." I was taken aback and speechless as I wanted so much to tell him I was not going to accept it. But how could I? He had that eager, little boy look on his face – how could I hurt his feelings?

So, I accepted the gift graciously.

"I am sure you will like it," he said, "I asked my mother to purchase it for me and she said, 'leave it to me, I know what young ladies' like'." He whispered to me, "It's 'lingerie'!"

Oh my god, I thought, what has he told his mum? I don't really know him, god, he's jumping the gun a bit, how am I going to get out of this one? After thinking of no end of excuses I decided to give it back to him tomorrow and I had visions of satin and delicate silk that lay in that box.

Part of me wanted to open it but when arriving in the billet, the task was taken out of my hands. Diana remarked, "You lucky so-and-so, what have you got that I haven't?"

"Search me," I replied, "and I have never even been out with him!"

"God, did you hypnotise the man?" Marge piped up, "It's her charm." They all jumped on my bed, "Come on Eve, open it up."

"Hold up," I said weakly, "I am going to give it back to him tomorrow."

"No, you damn well will not," said Diana, "you've got to open it up and if you don't like what's in there, then you can give it back!"

I gave in because I knew they would not let me out of there otherwise.

"Ah, that's a sport," said Joan. I undid the ribbon and stopped to read the card which said, 'Merry Christmas to a lovely lady, yours, Roy'.

"Oh, come on," they chorused, "open it up, we're all dying to see what's inside. With that posh gold and silver box there's bound to be something exciting in there!"

"Did you mention it was lingerie?" asked Diana. I nodded my head.

To my horror and amazement, after peeling back the tissue wrapping, I lifted out a pair of bright pink knickers, in Celanese (that awful starchy material) granny drawers, with elastic legs, I think they are called directoire knickers, and to cap it all, extra large! Diana burst out in peals of laughter, grabbed the drawers and put them on, stretching them so they came up to her neck. It was hilarious!

Nancy said, "Do you think that pair was just a joke, pull back some more layers, Evie." But lo and behold, the next one out was a long vest in bright pink, which Marge put on and it fell below her knees! So there they were, prancing around the room in 'granny's' undergarments! Then, to follow, was a pea-green set! I should never have opened that Pandora's box. My vision of silk and satin went down like a popped balloon. Well, he certainly was *not* a man of the world! With a present like that, it would have been better to leave it in the pretty box!

'Woe-is-me' Vera came rushing in while Marge and Diana were having high jinx, shouting, "What the hell are you mad lot up to in here? I will have you lot know that I am trying to have an intelligent conversation with my friend," and then looking over at Diana asked, "Where the hell did you get those passion killers from?"

"We are just trying them out for a fancy dress, Miss Nosy Parker," replied Marge, "Now, go back to your intelligent conversation and shut the door on your way out!"

"I want you all to promise me," I said, "not to breathe a word of this to your boyfriends or in the canteen. I should be mortified for Roy. After all, he most likely did not know what his mother had bought." Or maybe it was her way of putting me off her only son! Who knows!!

Last night I had one hell of a nightmare concerning the Christmas present from Roy. It went like this; Diana pranced around the bar in the pink bloomers and Marge joined her in the green pair, and there they were dancing the Can-Can with the troops urging them on. I opened my mouth to shout, "Please, please STOP!" but no sound escaped my lips. I tried to walk towards them but my body was frozen to the spot and I felt in a state of humiliation. I awoke in a panic, my heart thumping in my chest. What a relief to find it was only a dream! Then I began to fret about what to say to him when he comes into the canteen. Oh, why the hell did I accept the present? After all, it would have been much better to have left it in its pretty box. Now, I have to talk my way out of this and live in hope that Diana doesn't let me down.

We were very busy on the bar – a lot more new troops passing through. I was about to pull down the shutters when Roy came in.

"Ah, just caught you in time," he said.

Oh hell, I thought. "I am sorry," I said, "I am just closing up."

"I won't keep you," he replied, "I just wanted to know how you liked the present?"

"Oh, oh very nice," I stuttered, "many thanks!"

He carried on, "I just wondered, because my mother purchased them and also boxed them up for you. All I did was put the red ribbon on and sign the card. Did she choose well, Eve? She wouldn't let me see the undies, said it wouldn't be decent for a young man to look at them and it may give me ideas!"

Oh god, I thought, they, sure as hell would not excite anyone, they were just out and out passion killers! Give me strength, I thought, he is a mummy's boy and that is her way of putting a female off her darling son. If she only knew, there is not a cat in hell's chance with me even fancying him!

So as not to hurt his feelings I said to him, "Tell your mother they were perfect in every way and I will keep them for 'best'. Now I have to go Roy, so goodbye and have a merry Christmas." The memory of that nightmare will stay with me forever!

Home for Christmas; I always have that feeling when I return home, of being on the outside and looking in. Life changes in so many ways, although I did have a lovely time and ate too much. They are always trying to fatten me up, my Aunty Glad said I was too skinny! We went to see the pantomime Cinderella and my old school friend, Anna, came over and we went out to 'trip the light fantastic' on the dance floor of the Scala ballroom. I won a bracelet and my partner Andy, a bottle of whiskey. He was home on leave from the RAF and the prizes were for the Tango, my favourite dance. Anna hit it off well with his mate Charlie.

It was nice to be back at the NAAFI and I must confess I did miss them all. I have a busy week ahead as Miss Kitty is taking four days' leave and, help, I am in charge. She said, "You will be fine, I'm leaving it all in your capable hands."

It is very quiet around the place as Diana is on leave too. It is still very cold although no more snow and Fred the snowman is still on guard outside the billet. Nancy was emptying the soot from the flues of the ovens into the bin when a gust of wind blew a lot of it over him, so he is now a black and white snowman. There is not much left of Fred. He is sinking fast, for a while he had this amazing icicle hanging from his carrot nose just like a dewdrop!

That is one hell of a dirty job, cleaning out those flues in the kitchen. It is a thankless task, for if the ovens don't heat up to the cook's expectations, then poor Nancy takes the flack, even though she's done her job thoroughly. Then there is the 'filling up' of the coal buckets and carrying them up the steps and into the kitchen to stoke up the fire to heat the ovens ready for the cooks when they come on duty. Oh, and not forgetting to black-lead the large stove until it shines – we help her when we can, especially with the heavy buckets.

They are having a Social on camp at the weekend in the sergeants' mess, so I'm looking forward to that if all goes well. I have roped in Marge to help me in the office with the cashing-up – I just hope and pray that I can cope with all this responsibility!

My first day of being in charge did not go very well and I was rushed off my feet. Firstly, Joan asked if I had done the menus for the day.

"Menus?" I asked, "what menus?"

"For today!" was Joan's reply.

I stammered, "But I thought you did that."

"No, no," piped up Vera, "that's your job while Miss Kitty's away. Did she not brief you on that?" she asked with a smirk.

Lovely Joan said, "Come on, I'll help you, let's go in the office and I'll show you the ropes." I found that more difficult than spending a busy day on the bar! Everything had to be weighed and accounted for when getting the necessary ingredients from the stockroom, and the dreaded tea book drove me round the bend, every ounce of tea, sugar and milk was measured! Also, I had to carry around with me this enormous bunch of keys and had to open up the storeroom every time the cooks needed more ingredients and stay with either one of them while they weighed everything out.

It made me feel uncomfortable. No wonder Miss Kitty always said, "When you are in charge you have to keep your own counsel, no close friends and keep things on an even keel is my motto, Evie, then things run smoothly."

I am beginning to think I'm not very ecstatic about this job! Roll on the day that Miss Kitty returns to the fold. I doubt if I am cut out for this but I'll do my utmost to make it work. Joan was a great support; she said, "I can see you are worried, Evie, but don't be. We are all here to help you, just be yourself, you are stronger than you think!"

Today the padre came into the office when I was struggling with the invoices. I could see he was hankering after a cup of coffee and a chat, but I was at a loss at what to say. Every time I looked at him I had a vision of the tea party and Diana being a little devil and I had to suppress the urge to giggle at the thought of that funny episode. It turned out that he wanted a box of chocolates for his mother's birthday. He frantically searched his pockets for the money.

"So sorry," he blustered, "it seems the cupboard is bare, I will have to be in your debt for now. I'll bring it in, in the morning." Then, grabbing the chocolates from the desk, made a quick exit through the door. Later, I paid for them with my money!

My next visitor was the orderly officer and his request was for ciggies. He settled himself in the easy chair and asked, "What time is coffee break?"

I replied, "I haven't got time for that!"

"Oh, come on, young lady, all work and no play makes Jill a dull girl."

I turned to him and said, "I will send for one of the girls to bring in your cigarettes, how many packs and what brand would you like?"

"Benson and Hedges," he replied, "a twelve pack. Oh, and a box of chocolates with a winter scene, and," he added, grinning from ear to ear, "one cup of coffee and an Eccles cake!" He then proceeded to delve into his pocket and peeled out several notes, "Take it out of that," he said, gushing, "keep the change and put it into your staff fund."

Oh blast, I thought, I will have to let him stay now while he consumes his coffee and cake. The invoices will have to wait; I wondered who else would pay me a visit.

We have a new girl coming to replace Alice. Her name is Vickie Rhodes and apparently her nickname is Dusty, so the district manager informed me when he came in today. Personally, I think he was checking up on me, to make sure I was steering the ship on an even keel. He followed me around the place and as he never gave any indication of leaving I said to him, "Now, Mr Howarth, as we have the pleasure of your company today I'll leave you to hold the fort in the office while I go and help out on the bar, as they are run off their feet out there."

Looking at his watch he replied, "Make it half an hour only as I have an appointment in town."

I smiled at him and replied, "Half an hour then, on the dot!"

Josie, myself and Brenda, St Lucia, Borden

On the canteen bar at St Lucias Camp, Borden, with May

My Staff and me at Borden Camp, St Lucia

My husband Bill, far left, in Egypt on Christmas day

Chapter 10

1950 New Year. We are all feeling the worse for wear! Our celebration saw us 'tripping the light fantastic' at the Spa ballroom in Torquay. Diana came back early from leave to join us; it wouldn't have been the same without her. She met a very nice young man who is in the RAF whose name is Edward and was home on leave. Roger seems to be out of the picture lately. Margie said that she somehow knew it was a 'flash in the pan'! Miss Kitty is back on Saturday, so back to normal. I felt like a VIP today when the orderly corporal escorted me to the bank at the far end of the camp, to bank the takings. He was also 'on guard' inside the bank and awaiting my return with rifle slung over his shoulder. He spoke only two words; at the NAAFI it was, "Ready" and on departure from the bank it was "Ready". So I have nicknamed him 'Ready Eddie'!

The new girl, Dusty came today. She is a very pretty, dainty girl and very demure. She had been a chargehand at the other NAAFI that she had left, so was a great help in the office at cashing-up time. That let Joan off the hook which made 'woe is me' Vera happy to have her back full-time and to top it all she was a wizard with the dreaded tea book, much to my relief, as it was the bane of my life! Whoever invented that should come back and invent a better way of setting up – but I always managed it in the end even though it was so time consuming.

My birthday today – the great age of twenty-three years! Surprise, surprise, Vinnie made me a cake so we are all having a tea party later. Miss Kitty is back and it was great to pass the reins back over to her. I did not have to go on duty as I had been given the day off so the girls brought me my breakfast over on a tray to my bed and everyone had bought me a present. It was lovely – I felt so pampered! Diana and Marge had clubbed together to buy me black satin undies with a note inside which read 'In place of the passion killers!!' What a lovely gang they are. I am so pleased I found the NAAFI. It has opened up a new life for me and also enriched my life with all these wonderful characters.

Today, Miss Kitty inquired if there was anything to report on while she was away.

I replied, "The district manager, Mr Hawksworth visited but didn't stay long because he could see that we were busy. Orderly officer popped in to buy ciggies and chocolates and gave generously to our staff fund."

"What!" she said in surprise, "he actually gave a tip?!"

"Yes," I replied.

"What the hell did you do to him?"

"Nothing, nothing at all, just smiled sweetly!"

"Well, I will have to let you deal with him in future," she said.

"No thanks, I'll leave that to you," I replied.

Alice is back. She looks radiant (still not smoking) and we have her for a few more weeks before she goes to Germany. Life is back to normal.

We are very busy with a new influx of troops so it is the usual Blanco, boot polish etc. I received a letter today from Andy, one of the lads that went out to Korea. He describes the conditions out there as hell on earth, not only the enemy but also the flies and mosquitoes. He went on to say that many of his group were suffering from various fevers and that he had been on guard duty for two nights and was dreading it. He said, 'please give my love to all the NAAFI girls, we all miss you and oh god, wish we were back in lovely Devon. We are all in need of pen-pals so I am enclosing a list of names. It will give us all something to look forward to in this godforsaken place and P.S. send us a photo of you all. Forgive the fly-spattered paper – the blasted things are swarming in the tent.'

I have put the letter on the notice board in the kitchen, so soon many letters will be wending their way to those dear lads. We are also all going to contribute to a parcel for them all.

Today four Yanks came into the canteen. Their names were Elmer, Lee, Pope and Ches. They made a beeline for Diana's bar and there she was fluttering her eyelashes – the minx! The very tall one called Pope said to Diana, "Hiya honey, yer sure have gold in them there hills!"

Saucily she asked, "Got any gum, chum?"

"Anything for you, honey," he replied.

I could see things were getting out of hand and there was a lot of murmuring from our troops. I felt I had to nip it in the bud somehow but I had a hell of a queue myself at that present time. Miss Kitty came on to the bar just then and ordered Diana to go into the kitchen and help the cooks.

"Well, young men, what can I do for you?" she asked them.

"We would like four cups of coffee and four doughnuts please Ma'am," he replied,

"Are you staying on camp long?" enquired Miss Kitty.

"We sure would like to stay longer, it sure is wonderful scenery around this neck of the woods, but much to our regret we are moving up north soon, Ma'am," he replied.

Later, Miss Kitty had a word with Diana, "You are treading a dangerously thin line, young lady, when will you ever learn?!!"

Today there was not a lot to do before opening the bar so we all went into the canteen for our break, armed with coffee and hot scones just out of the oven. Joan joined us there and we sat looking out over the parade ground.

The sergeant major was shouting out his commands and one poor recruit dropped his rifle, so had to endure a torrent of abuse from him. The poor lad didn't look very old and he called him 'a weak-willed poofter'.

"What's a poofter?" asked Ruby.

Diana raised her eyes and said, "You know, it's one of those things you rest your feet on!"

Ruby asked, "But why would he want to put his feet up?"

"Leave it be, Rube," Diana replied, "look it up in the dictionary!"

To our amazement there was hilarious movement in the ranks. The recruits were marching up and down all over the place and some were doing the German goose step. We watched, ever closer to the window, to see what was going on. Lo and behold, the sergeant major had got his jaw stuck! It was as though he was paralysed and his mouth was wide open. This went on for a good ten minutes, during which the antics of the troops was so funny. Then, as if by magic he came back to normal. He shook his head from side to side, the recruits quickly got back into line and stood there like statues and he called over to his corporal, "Get this 'orrible lot off the square and lead them on a two-mile march. The ringleaders I'll have in the 'glasshouse' – I'll give them goose step!" And with that, he tucked his stick under his arm and marched off.

Ruby offered her discovery that she now knew what the 'glasshouse' was. "What's that, Rube?" asked Joan.

"A house made of glass!" was her reply made in all innocence and with a look of enlightenment on her face.

Diana said, "We are so pleased about that, Rube, but it is one of those places where you would not like to go!"

"But, why? Would it be horrible?" Ruby asked.

"Forget it, come on and let's pull up the shutters. We have the troops to feed and water." Ruby walked away with a look of bewilderment on her pretty face.

Roy, the passion killer man, came in today. I tried my utmost to avoid him but to no avail, he was still eager to know how I liked the lingerie. I told him it was very nice.

"Can we go out on a date sometime?" he asked with an eager look on his face, which gave me the creeps!

"So sorry," I replied sharply, "but I have a boyfriend."

"But you never mentioned that!" he replied.

"Well, you never asked did you, Roy?"

"Is he on the camp?" he enquired.

"Yes," I lied.

"Oh dear, I am so sorry, I just assumed you were unattached," he replied. And with that he made a beeline for Diana's bar and started chatting her up. Now that should be interesting!

Yesterday afternoon Marge, Diana, Alice, Ruby and I went on a bike ride. We borrowed bikes from various quarters; mine was a sit-up-and-beg bike with a basket on the front in which I ended up carrying all the girls' bags. I joked that I would cycle away into the sunset with all their dosh!

Diana had a man's bike and it was so funny when she tried to mount it as she had to cock her leg over the bar. After several attempts she eventually managed it, but then complained like mad that there was something in the saddle that was sticking up her backside, and that every time she moved the saddle went too. We were all beginning to think that we would never get anywhere on this ride. Margie's bike was a drop-handled racing cycle, so we were a real assortment!

Diana suggested that we call in at the farm and visit Roger, so that was our first port of call. Roger and his dad were herding the cattle in to the milking sheds when we all arrived. Diana was finding dismounting from her bike impossible, so with great laughter from Roger's dad, he came over and lifted her off saying, "What scrap yard did you get this bike from?"

"The camp!!" we all chorused. When he lifted Diana the seat moved upright. My descent was not very ladylike either as I caught the hem of my skirt in the front of the saddle, although I was more worried about laddering my new silk stockings! I called out for help and Ruby removed the offending skirt from the seat saying, "You could do with a stitch in that, we'll call in at my gran's on the way and she'll fix it for you." I was beginning to wonder if that cycle ride had been a good idea!

Diana was asked by Roger if she would like to try her hand at milking.

"Not likely," was her answer, "but Eve is a good milker, she was in the Land Army during the War." Thanks very much, Diana, I thought as Roger asked me if I would give them a 'demo'.

"Well, I don't think so!" I replied.

"Oh go on, Evie!" they all chorused. So there I was milking a cow called Maisie and when I handed over the bucket of milk to Roger, I was quite pleased with myself for not forgetting my dairy skills which I had learnt on the land.

We all enjoyed our visit to Ruby's gran; she is a lovely lady, although how we got there down those winding lanes is a mystery to me. Diana fell off her bike several times and one time we had to drag her out of a ditch, covered in mud. Of course, she blamed it on the saddle even though Roger's dad had fixed it for her. We all cycled as far away from her as we could as she wobbled all over the place and at times had great difficulty reaching the pedals. She declared to Ruby's gran that her arse was sore and she was sure she had suffered some dreadful injury from the bloody bike! Ruby's gran laughed so much, she farted! Poor old dear, the piece of fruit cake she was eating at the time very nearly choked her! I patted her back and the cake crumbs just cascaded from the corners of her mouth! She retorted, "You girls are a real tonic, come back soon to see me. Don't you forget, Ruby love, bring them over again soon!"

When we got back to camp Diana complained that she felt like she had been riding a horse and she was sure that one leg had fallen out with the other!

Chapter 11

Elsie is in great form and is as pleased as punch that her posting has come through and she is off to Germany in a week. Vinnie is also leaving us and his destination is Port Said. We have a new girl from Glasgow arriving at the weekend. So, it is all change here and Margie remarked that Diana will miss her old sparring partner – it certainly won't be the same.

Ruby informed us all that there is a dance in the village hall tomorrow night so we have decided to give it a go. It will make a change from the camp socials.

One big problem is that we don't finish our stint on the bar until 9.30pm. Vinnie's verdict is, "You are all crazy, by the time you get there it will be time to come back and the orderly officer locks the main gates at midnight." But we can get over that problem by using the escape route at the back of the billets through a hole in the hedge. But we do have to cross a field to get there! Diana says it will be a doddle, and she should know having used it many times. At least, it will be an adventure! But, I will make sure I take my pumps as I don't fancy the idea of walking across a field in my court shoes, and not forgetting a torch too.

Little Nancy is away on sick leave, so we are all taking it in turns to do the fires in the kitchen, lugging in coal and cleaning out the dreaded flues. All that soot to scoop up, I do hope the wind is in the right direction when it's my turn. I don't fancy it blowing in my face when I'm emptying it into the bin!

Valentine's Day and to my great surprise I received three cards. Diana and Marge were awaiting me to open them up so with great anticipation and wondering who, I opened them. The words on the first said, 'I am so lonesome without you, what am I to do?' and signed 'R'. I will not repeat my reaction to that one! The second one said, 'Will you be my sweetheart? I admire you from afar' and signed John. I have not got a clue who that could be! The third is a creepy one which read, 'I seek you here, I seek you there, I *will* seek you anywhere' and was signed – guess who? My thoughts on that one was that it was the 'Psycho' military policeman. Marge joked, "It could be the Scarlet Pimpernel!" Diana has received four, so she is dancing around the billet much to the annoyance of 'woe-is-me Vera' and Margie received one from Lance. We all sent a card to Vinnie, so he's in a quandary about who it's from, especially as we had given it to one of the recruits who was on his way to Catterick camp to post!

The dance at the village hall last night mostly consisted of the village locals and we soon realised they were accompanied by the mothers and grans etc. They all sat around the room keeping their beady eyes on their precious sons and pursing their lips like chicken bums, giving us all the evil eye! The atmosphere was electric and Diana was all for livening the place up! Ruby's gran was there sitting in the far corner and her gummy smile welcomed us over to sit with her. As we walked past the village folk they made it obvious we were not welcome; there they were tutting and huddled together whispering. We remarked to gran, whatever was their problem? She replied, "They have more beak than bum!" We laughed.

"What does that funny saying mean?" I asked.

"Well m'dear, they are just nosey and um don't know which way their backside hangs out!"

I looked at Ruby and she said, "Don't ask!"

"She's just a lovely character," I replied.

I expect they thought that as we worked on an army camp that we weren't good enough for their precious sons to dance with, but looking over the local talent, they surely wouldn't have any worry on that score.

The band was from the local RAF station and they were good, but when they left the hall for a break an elderly fellow came on to entertain us playing the ancient piano. He puffed away furiously on a Woodbine cigarette, which he moved around his mouth with sparks cascading from his lips and his eyes screwed up tightly from the smoke which enclosed around him. He thumped away on the ivories as though his life depended upon it, bashing away on the pedals with gusto. The old grannies called out to him to play their favourites, "Come on, Fred lad, let's have 'Run Rabbit Run'."

"Bloody hell," Diana retorted, "I wish they would all sod off and chase the rabbits!" so she went over to him and asked if he would play 'In the Mood'.

"I dunno that one, gal," said Fred, so she sat beside him and said, "Move over, Fred, I'll start and you follow!" As if by magic, the youth of the village all got onto the dance floor and jived. Diana and Fred tickled those ivories to the sheer amazement of us all, we were so surprised by Diana's hidden talent. She'd certainly kept that one quiet. So, when the band returned they played all our favourites including the tango, quickstep, jive etc. On looking over at the mums and grans, much to my surprise they all seemed to be enjoying it too.

When the band struck up the music of a tango, a very short, spotty youth came over and asked me to dance. How could I refuse, with the beady eyes of the locals upon me? He proceeded to bounce around like a jack-in-the-box, his head going in all directions. I was more worried about where his head was going than with him stepping on my feet. His legs were going like pistons and he delved into his pocket and pulled out a grey piece of rag with which he proceeded to mop his brow. God knows what else it had been used for.

"Ah, that be better," he said, "it ain't arf 'ot in 'ere, gal!" His breathing was laboured and when the music stopped he was panting. Never, in all my life, have I seen the tango danced like that!

A rather large lady called out to him angrily, "Get over here now, Percy!"

I said, "You'd better go or you'll be in the dog house," and he slunk away.

The main gates were locked when we eventually got back so we made our way across the field, a journey I would not like to repeat. It was pitch black and my small torch did nothing to help light our way. Marge put her foot in a cow pat and Diana said she was sure that there was a bull in the field because she could hear something snorting!

"Well, I don't think so, Diana, as he would have charged us by now," I retorted, "and after all it would be very difficult for him to see what he was charging at in the dark!"

"I bloody well know that," she replied, "I am more worried about bumping into him!" We found the hole in the hedge with great difficulty and Diana was in a hell of a mood because she had laddered her stockings.

On reaching the billet, we tapped on the window. 'Woe is me' Vera poked her head out and shouted, "Why should I let you mad lot in?" I put my hand over Diana's mouth because I guessed it would be abusive and I did not fancy sleeping outside. So with moans and groans 'Woe is me' let us in.

This morning Diana was relating to Vinnie about the phantom bull and his answer was, "You would have known if it had been a bull when you got his horns up your arse!" Marge and I chuckled, we will miss him and his wisecracks when he leaves.

It was very busy today with a new batch of recruits on camp whose mission would eventually be Korea. I sold mostly Blanco, Brasso, boot polish and dusters. Eager young lads, all thinking they are starting on a new adventure. My heart went out to them, when will it all end? The kitchen is a hive of activity with the cooking of tray after tray of pastries, Eccles cakes and meat pies. We have two young recruits in the kitchen helping out with spud-bashing. They are both on 'jankers' for going AWOL.

I am on early tomorrow morning doing my stint of cleaning out the flues of the stove and as I think of poor Nancy doing it day in and day out I make a silent plea, 'hurry back, Nancy, before I lose the will to live!' Marge said she will help me bring in the coal – I am sure I am going to end up with muscles like Popeye!

This morning at 6.45 I dragged myself out of bed, thinking that I must be mad letting myself in for this. The billet was freezing cold and the wind was gusting outside rattling the windows and roaring down the chimney like a monster. Diana was snoring away and grinding her teeth. Marge was talking in her sleep and said something that sounded like, 'Yes, yes we will, we will run away!' Although shivering I waited to hear more, but to no avail, just a lot of mumbling. I must remember to ask her what she was dreaming, it sure sounded interesting. My mind went into overdrive – perhaps she has a secret lover! I donned my oversize overall, tied a piece of string around the waist and wrapped a red check tea cloth around my head. I happened to glance at my vision in the mirror on my way out and frightened myself, so I hope no one else is around when I go outside or they will think that the Arabs have invaded! Everything went well and I cleaned out the flues, lit the fires, brought in the coal, swept up and ran the black lead brush around the black stoves. No sign of Marge, 'I'll help with the coal buckets,' she had said. Perhaps she ran off with her lover from her dream!

As I had finished early I decided to do my good deed for the day and take them all a nice cup of tea in bed. Was that a good idea? No! They all moaned that I had woken them too early. Marge said, "You scared the hell out of me, what are you dressed up like that for and you're covered in soot. When you woke me all I could see was the whites of your eyes – and where the bloody hell did you get the headgear from?"

"Thanks," I retorted, "and where the hell were you, after all you did promise to help me."

"Oh did I?" she replied, yawning, "well big deal, I forgot!"

"Would you like your tea over your head?" I asked, and with that she rolled over and went back to sleep! Lesson one, no good deeds before breakfast – ever! I had a good soak in the bath then went up to the kitchen to help the cooks with the breakfast. Joan was pleased that the fires were going well and the ovens heating up.

"How about taking it on until Nancy gets back?" she asked.

"No thanks," I replied, "once is enough and I'm allergic to soot! Anyway it is Margie's turn tomorrow and she is so looking forward to doing it!" I said. (Like hell!)

Fred the snowman is no more – his remains were swept away yesterday.

Later on this morning I am going out in the NAAFI van to serve refreshments to the troops who are on manoeuvres out in the countryside and my driver is none other than Vinnie. I am looking forward to it. This morning, Marge brought me over tea and biscuits in bed and left me a note on the tray which said, "Sorry, see you when you get back." Diana is on day off so she was in the land of nod when I left. Vinnie had stocked up the van and collected the float. It was quite an interesting day, although to start with we had a bit of difficulty with the tea urn. The tap would just not turn on and there were all the recruits chomping at the bit. Vinnie nearly blew a gasket and the air was blue, but then one of the lads came to the rescue and in two seconds flat he had fixed it and we were in business.

Today, we helped Alice with her packing. She is off tomorrow to be with Archie. We will miss her. The new girl, Maggie, came today and is billeted in the next room with 'woe is me

Vera'. She is a tall very slender girl with a mass of shiny black curly hair, very attractive and must be nigh on 6 foot tall.

Even at my 5ft 6ins I feel like a midget beside her! I also find it difficult to understand her broad Scottish accent – she called me 'her wee hen'!

Nancy is back, so we all breathed a sigh of relief, no more stoking the fires in the kitchen.

Marge and I are off modelling at the weekend for Bobbies fashion store in Torquay. Miss Kitty remarked, "You two girls are in great demand. Are we going to lose you?"

"Not at all," I replied, "it's only temporary, in the afternoons when there is a problem with their regular models through sickness or family traumas."

"That reminds me, Eve, I have something to talk over with you," she said, "not urgent, but when you have a spare ten minutes in your off-duty time."

My, what can that be, I thought. Vinnie, who had been earwigging said, "I think, maybe you are being posted. Now that would put the cat amongst the pigeons with your nice little earner on the modelling front!"

"Oh, get lost, Vinnie," I replied. I am ignoring that remark. At times I despair with him, he is a complex character, sometimes funny and kind and then on the other hand downright nasty.

Maggie's first day on the bar caused quite a stir among the troops. They all flocked to her bar to be served, some giving her the chat-up line and her response was, "My wee men, did yer ken, I would have to look down on you. Away you go and chat up another bonnie lassie!" It was amusing to watch, with all their flattery they were not getting very far with Maggie!

We were quite busy in the canteen today with another bunch of new recruits and I soon emptied my shelves of ciggies, boot polish and Blanco. Ruby came to help me out to stock up and refill my shelves.

Ruby told me a funny story today; it was about when she went to stay on holiday with her dad's mother in Manchester. She said her gran lived in a cottage near a railway line. They had no inside toilet, it was a bucket lav at the bottom of the garden in a wooden shed. Ruby told me that her gran was a canny old dear, she had all the times of the trains and knew exactly when the coal train came along the track. So, she would tell Ruby to get down to the lav and to sit on the toilet seat with the door open. "But why?" asked Ruby.

"Just do it," her gran said, "and take this bucket with you."

"But why?" Ruby asked again.

"You'll see, quick I can hear it coming," she said.

Ruby sat on the toilet just as she had been told, with the door open and as the train went by the men threw lumps of coal at her, which landed on the floor at her feet. I remarked that some of it could have hit her but she said that it didn't and, "then I realised what the bucket was for and filled it up with the coal." Gran was so pleased, we were able to stoke up the fire and warm up the cottage.

"But, why didn't your gran do what everyone else does and have the coalman?" I asked.

"There was a coal shortage and it was rationed," she said.

I didn't ask any more – I've heard it all now!! I can't get that image out of my mind of Ruby sitting on the lav with the door open to the elements and the 'coalmen' throwing it at her!!

Chapter 12

Miss Kitty's little talk rather took me by surprise. I am being posted to Bridgenorth in Shropshire, a Royal Air Force camp where I am being employed as a chargehand for two months. She has promised that I will return saying, "Think of it as experience, Eve." So here I go again on my travels to pastures new. Marge is upset about it, but after all two months is not long. My home town, Worcester is not all that far from Bridgenorth so I will be able to get home more often.

Miss Kitty said, "It will be a good time for you to leave at the weekend. Then you can spend two days with your family before you report to RAF Bridgenorth on Tuesday of next week."

I said my goodbyes to the girls and Vinnie unexpectedly gave me a great bear hug and a kiss. I wished him well on his posting to the desert.

Miss Kitty decided it would be much better for me to travel to the station in her old Austin 7. She said it would be much more comfortable than Rick's 'bone-rattler'. Well, I was not so sure about that! Vinnie gave the old banger a good crank up and it sputtered and banged and rattled. It sounded to me that the exhaust was on its last legs and I thought, if we get to the station it will be a miracle!

Diana insisted on coming along, so we set off for the station. Miss Kitty was having trouble with the gears and there was this awful smell of burning oil!

We chugged along the country lanes leaving a trail of smoke behind us. I was glad that Diana had decided to come along as she would be an extra hand at pushing it if we broke down. I thought, what a journey! We arrived at the station in a cloud of smoke and Miss Kitty asked Diana to help me with my luggage. She opened up the bonnet of the old girl to let her cool down and when I looked back I saw her in a haze of steam.

Well, here I am at HQ NAAFI, RAF camp. On meeting Miss Harp, the manageress, I was filled with dread. My god, she is an overpowering woman. She is a tall, well-built woman in her mid-forties at a guess, brassy blonde hair, heavy features, wears heavy make-up and bright red lipstick.

The perfume she uses smells of Ashes of Roses and wafted around her, mingled in the air with cigarette smoke from the gold-tipped holder that she puffed away on. I share a room with a girl named Jean, a pretty, petite blonde with deep-blue eyes. Two more girls in the next room, Polly and Esme and then there is the cook Annie, a cheerful and bubbly woman.

That is the entire staff – a much smaller canteen than at Denbury but I did notice that the ovens are more up-to-date – oil-fired I think, so no more cleaning flues! Oh, and a lady called Lily comes in from the village every day to help Annie in the kitchen.

My duties are part-time on the net bar and helping out in the office with 'Glamour Puss', Miss Harp. Polly is a bouncy little girl, full of life and not unlike Diana. Esme is the exact opposite, very shy and quiet, she is tall and willowy with deep-brown eyes and long chestnut-brown hair that cascades down her back in waves. Miss Harp is forever telling Esme to tie it back when she serves on the bar, but to no avail, she just tosses her head and ignores her, and never utters a word just calmly carries on!

It was my first day on the net bar this morning; I found the RAF recruits very reserved and a doddle to serve and there was no pushing and shoving in the queues.

Cashing-up in the office I did not enjoy, especially with 'Glamour Puss' puffing away on her ciggies. There was one hell of a fug in there, and with her heavy perfume mingled with the smoke, I did not linger long. She wanted me to stay and talk but I made the excuse that I needed to do my ironing. She called after me as I was departing through the door, "Be a dear, Eve, and collect mine from my room and run the iron over it."

Oh god, I thought, here we go again, I have let myself in for something. I'll have to be careful or she will have me doing her washing as well – crafty madam!! Jean remarked, "She is a real bag of tricks, beware!"

I'm just about getting into the swing of things here and went into the town of Bridgenorth with Polly yesterday afternoon. I really enjoyed my time there and decided to go back soon and do some more sightseeing in the near future. We were invited to a social evening at the ergeants' mess last night and Polly introduced me to an air gunner named Don. We got on like a house on fire, owing to the fact that his home town was Worcester, so we had that in common. It was great and I have a date to go to the cinema in town with him next week. He is tall and handsome – this place is certainly getting more interesting! Polly said, "Take my advice, don't tell 'Glamour Puss' or she will put the kibosh on it!"

When I asked why, she replied, "That is what she's like – thinks that every man should drop at her feet!"

"In other words, she's a man eater!" I remarked. I am getting to learn more and more about our manageress. Oh well, I am only here for a short time and at least it isn't as hectic as Denbury.

I received a letter today from the gang at Denbury. They said, hurry back we are missing you, and all sent me a kiss – even 'woe is me Vera' – now that's a first! They have a new cook in the kitchen to replace Vinnie, her name is Amy. Diana says, there is no one to spar with and that all is quiet on the western front!

When I get the opportunity I must go for a walk around the countryside here. The camp is quite out in the sticks but the view from the billet window was breathtaking, with the pale sunshine glistening over the frosted fields and hedgerows. The RAF band were practising their music this morning on the parade ground. They looked so smart and well turned out.

This morning I was making my way across the Green to post letters in the pillar box, when from nowhere this sergeant major appeared, strutting along with his stick tucked neatly under his arm and he bellowed at me, "Get off that bloody grass! Now!" I was rooted to the spot, uncertain whether to turn back or carry on. Being half way across I kept going, while he stood there watching me, posted the letters and then headed for the roadway. I could feel his eyes boring into my back as I walked towards the canteen. Well, I have just learnt that the RAF sergeants are the same breed as the Army ones!

No wonder the recruits jump to it when they appear on the scene.

Amy asked me today if I would like to go with her to the riding stables which are nearby here. "Why?" I asked.

"Well, it's like this," she said, "There is a groom there that I rather fancy and, Eve, I don't really want to go on my own so do come with me," she pleaded.

Against my better judgement I replied, "Oh alright then, I will."

We arrived at the stables at about 2.30pm and Amy was all aglow, "There he is, look," she said excitedly, "Is he not handsome?"

"Oh, yeah," I replied, lying through my teeth. I'm going to regret this, I thought as he came striding towards us.

"My, my, what have we here?" he enthused in a sugary voice, "two lovely ladies!"

He was thin and scrawny with black hair that was pasted smooth to his scalp, with ferrety eyes that darted around like a bird.

"Now, now what brings you two to my neck of the woods?" he asked. Amy replied, "We thought it would be a good idea to come and look at the ponies."

"Well, my goodness me, your luck is in as we have several new ones in the stables," he replied, "Come on, don't be shy," he said, looking straight at me, "they don't bite, and ha ha, neither do I!" That, I thought, remains to be seen. "Oh, by the by, my name is Silas."

Amy piped up, fluttering her eyelashes at him, "My name is Amy," and pointing at me, "and that is Eve." Looking over at me he said, "And is there an Adam?"

"Well," I said, "as a matter of fact there is!"

"Oh blast," he said, smirking, "and there I was hoping my luck was in!"

In your dreams, I thought. Amy looked over at me and scowled. I practically had to drag her away from that place and on the way back she didn't utter one word! I think I had burst her bubble, but I like to think that I had saved her from that creep, slippery Silas! But then, I did fall in love with those lovely ponies especially a dapple grey one called Poppy. He did say that I could go back some time and take her out, but I declined on the grounds that I wouldn't trust that creep an inch!

A very funny episode occurred early this morning. I was making my way across to the canteen when I heard this almighty thud. Looking back, I saw Flight Commander Allcock hanging upside down outside Miss Harp's bedroom window. He had caught his jacket sleeve on the window ledge and was having great difficulty releasing it. I was tempted to go over and help him out but decided it would be too much of an embarrassment for him! So I hid inside the doorway and watched at a safe distance. It was so funny, I had to stifle my giggles but he managed at last to release the offending sleeve. Then I noticed that when he stood up he was as bald as a badger!

Next, he was on his hands and knees searching for his 'rug' (wig). I could see it from where I was standing, stuck between the wood panels of the billet – it looked like a furry animal! At last, after some tugging, he released it, slapped it on his head and I could see it was all skew-whiff. He did look funny, like somebody out of a comedy act. Then he dusted himself down, put on his cap and proceeded to limp away between the billets, looking about from left to right to make sure that no one saw him. Poor old Wingco, he did suffer for his night of passion! I do hope it was worth it!

Later, lying in bed recalling the incident, or should I say fiasco, I couldn't help chuckling softly at the very thought of it. At the breakfast table the following morning, Polly remarked, "That was a very amusing dream you were having last night. I could hear you chuckling away."

"Yes, it was, Polly, very funny!" I answered.

"Tell us then," they chorused.

"No, I don't think so!" I replied, I think I'll keep that one a secret!!

Very busy again on the bar with so many more new recruits on the scene, buying their essentials for their kit. There will be plenty of spit and polish for them to look forward to, before they pass before the sergeant major – sooner them than me. I've managed to have yet another fight with that dreaded tea book. I will never get the hang of it, no matter how hard I sweat over it. Miss Harp said, "I cannot see what you find so difficult. It is simple!" Well, I thought, you do it then!!

We have an invitation to the sergeants' mess on Saturday night, after the NAAFI is closed.

"Just get back by 11.30 sharp or you will be locked out," Miss Harp informed us. She has been in a very prickly mood of late and Jean told me that Romeo Wingco was on leave.

Diana rang last night which bucked me up no end. She said, "Hurry up and get back here, we all miss you. Even Miss Kitty is regretting sending you and said she would try and pull some strings for you to return!"

In a way I am pleased, but in another way I am just beginning to enjoy it here now I have settled in. I find 'pastures new' getting quite interesting and I have met some lovely characters in the young recruits. I have quite a following in the 'agony aunt' position! Miss Harp remarked to me, "I think, young lady, you have missed your vocation in life. Especially when I see those young lads walk out of the canteen with a smile on their face and a spring in their step. You certainly are doing something right, I'm just not sure what!"

Yesterday a tragic accident happened. One of the new recruits electrocuted himself and died. He was pressing his uniform in his billet and had plugged the iron into a low ceiling light. The medic said that he had been splashing water all over the place and was also standing in it. Poor lad, he was only twenty and had only been in the RAF six weeks, just on the dawn of his National Service.

We all enjoyed a great night at the sergeants' social and I met some great characters. The older airmen, pilots and air gunners were all 'rather rather', it was all 'Wacko' and everything was 'a piece of cake' and they referred to each other as 'Bods' and seemed to have a language of their own. And not forgetting those huge handlebar moustaches which curled up at the ends, which they stroked and teased as if they were their pet animals. It is beyond me how they didn't have their own private bonfires while they puffed on their pipes showering sparks all around. One such character made a beeline for me across the room. He was an air gunner but to describe his features is impossible because he was surrounded by smoke and sparks. His build was stocky and height, I would say, about five foot eight inches and from the way he walked across the room he had most probably downed a few bevies! As he approached me he said, still sucking on the old pipe, "Well, my lovely gal, what about we trip the light fantastic?"

I stuttered and stammered.

"Come on now, sweetie, I don't bite, it will be a piece of cake!" he continued.

"Well," I replied, nearly choking on his smoke, "get rid of that damned pipe and I'll think about it."

He proceeded to tap the offending pipe on the heel of his shoe and grind the contents into the floor. He brushed the ash from his tunic, straightened himself up and said, "Well, do I pass muster now or could there be something else?" Shoving his pipe into his tunic pocket, we hit the floor to do the foxtrot.

The band then struck up and announced an 'excuse me' dance, so I ended up dancing with some very handsome fellows and lost poor old 'Bod'. He never did tell me his name!

Towards the end of the evening Miss Harp decided to join us.

"Bloody hell," said Polly, "now she will keep her beady eyes on us, and I have met this gorgeous chap and he so wants to walk me back to the billet. I have a good idea, Eve."

"Oh yeah," I said, "what's that?"

"Well, you go over and keep her company," she said, "and then I can slip out with him."

"Afraid not," I retorted, "as a matter of fact I have met someone too. So go and ask one of the others, I'm sure they will oblige."

She sniffed, "They're too scared of her!" Why me then, I thought

His name is Mark and not much to relate at present but I'm hoping there will be – we have a date tomorrow afternoon.

Miss Harp was in a foul mood this morning and everybody seemed to be walking on eggshells. I asked Polly if she knew what was going on and she whispered, "Tell you later!"

I was putting out the floats, ready for opening up at lunchtime when Miss Harp stormed in behind me. "Well," she said angrily, eyes flashing, "when are you meeting him then?"

"Who?" I asked innocently, "I don't know what you mean."

"Come off it, I saw you last night deep in conversation with him."

"I am still at a loss as to what you are insinuating," I replied. By this time, I was getting really angry; how dare she question me on my private time away from the NAAFI. Who the hell does she think she is?

"Miss Harp," I said calmly, although inside I was seething, "we will end this conversation now. I will now pull up the shutters and get down to serving the airmen. After all, that's what I am here for, is it not?"

Without another word she stormed off with a trail of smoke behind her as she puffed furiously on the cigarette holder! Ah well, it looks as though I've cooked my goose and will be getting my marching orders!

Later Miss Harp and I cashed-up in complete silence. On my way out she called out, "Enjoy your afternoon, Eve."

I answered back, "I sure will!" Oh my, she is just one crazy mixed-up woman! I'm pleased, in a way, that I'm on a short term.

Mark was waiting outside camp for me. He is handsome in a rugged way with deep-blue eyes, blond wavy hair and tall. He was wearing a very smart dark-grey suit, blue shirt with a dark-blue RAF tie and when he smiles his eyes twinkle. Oh lordy, here I go again, smitten! We caught the Air Force bus into Bridgenorth and went sightseeing around the town. I felt as if I had known him forever! Over tea and cake in the local café he told me about his great hobby, which is painting with oils and also poetry. We have so much in common. Apparently he was the Education Officer on camp.

At the weekend we are meeting again as Mark said there is a good film on at the camp cinema. It's a musical, 'When I'm Calling You' starring Nelson Eddie and Jeanette McDonald.

Jean and Polly remarked that I had hit the jackpot being asked out by Mark.

"We are all green with envy!" "He is one hell of a catch!" "Best looking chap on Camp!" "But, just watch out for 'Glamour Puss', she has been lusting after him since he arrived on camp!" they warned.

"But, what about Wing Co?" I asked.

They laughed out loud, "He doesn't come into it, he is just one of many!"

"Well," I said, "Mark is far too young for her."

"That won't stop her, age doesn't come into it," they replied, "She thrives on the excitement of the chase, so Eve, beware!" Now I know why she was 'off' with me, oh dear, oh dear, looks like I will have to tread carefully. I have that awful feeling that there is trouble ahead!

The orderly officer came in today. Their mess have organised a social evening and would like us to do the buffet, drinks etc.

and serve behind their bar. The latter part of the evening we can partake in their celebrations. The girls are excited and already planning what they are going to wear. Miss Harp is full of high spirits and seems to have forgotten our little spat. Whilst cashing-up the takings in the office she divulged to me that I was to be in charge of the bar and buffet, 'because it would be time out for her, to mingle with the officers.'

"When is this social?" I asked.

"Tuesday evening," was her reply, "and just remember, the girls and you will be quite busy through the evening so really there won't be a lot of time left for you or any of the others to dance." I ignored this and remembered what my auntie's advice was, 'Never snap back when people annoy you, just kill them with kindness and they will be putty in your hands.'

So I put it to the test, "What are you going to wear, Miss Harp?" I asked smiling at her.

There was surprise on her face and she said, "I thought I would wear my black evening dress."

"Oh you will look beautiful in that," I replied, "with your blonde hair and fair skin you will 'wow' those officers!"

"My, my," she replied, "you are a sweet girl, Eve!" She practically purred like a pussycat, "I will have a dress rehearsal later, will you come to my room to give me your approval?" she purred.

"Of course I will, certainly," I replied, "It will be my pleasure."

On getting back to the billet I punched the air with my fist and muttered, "Got you, Tiger!" end of scene 1!

Today we were short-staffed with two girls down with the flu. Miss Harp is in a tizzy because of the impending officers 'do' and she asked me if I thought that they were skiving.

"Certainly not," I replied, "in fact, Jean is not at all well and I think she has a temperature."

"Just go and get a packet of Beechams powders from your net bar and mix one up for her. That should do the trick!" she said. So there I was playing nursie, I do have some amazing roles to play here!

This morning everything was quiet and Miss Harp's day off. Jean looks a lot better and was able to eat the breakfast I brought over for her. Esme is feeling better too and will be back on duty tomorrow. So my dosing them up with the Beechams did the trick, and my role of nursie will soon be over! Tomorrow we have a lady called Marian from the village coming to help out.

There seems to be a lot of activity going on around camp and rumours of a 'bigwig' visiting. It must be someone of importance as they have the whitewash out and everything seems to be getting a makeover – even the flagpole! The recruits were even out at the back of our kitchen moving the bins out of sight.

This afternoon I had a date with Mark and had arranged to meet him outside the canteen as we had planned to go to the camp cinema. But, lo and behold, he didn't turn up and it was so embarrassing standing there waiting.

Polly and Esme said, "Come on, Eve, come with us, we're going to the flicks," so I joined them and promised to give him a piece of my mind when I did see him.

Two days have gone by and no sign of Mark. I did ask after him, thinking perhaps that he had been taken ill, but none of the recruits had seen him around and one of them remarked, "He's probably gone AWOL!"

Very indignantly, I replied, "He wouldn't do that!"

They laughed, "That's what you think. He's done it before. I expect he's on a bender!"

I dismissed this as 'just gossip'. I have learnt since working in the NAAFI that men are worse than women on that score.

Marian was a good help today, I do hope Miss Harp keeps her on. She is so pretty with dark wavy hair down to her shoulders and is a great hit with the recruits, but is married to one of the sergeants on camp and they live in married quarters nearby.

Still no sign of Mark so maybe they were right about him.

Miss Harp was not very well today so I had the task of taking her breakfast in bed. I also had to collect the keys for the office and store room. There she was sitting up in bed, made up to the nines with her hair piled up on her head with diamanté combs and wearing a pink satin bed jacket. She did not look very sick to me!

"How are you?" I asked, "would you like me to get you a Beechams powder?"

"Not likely," she replied, "I don't want any of that muck but a brandy would not go amiss! I want you to do me a favour, my dear, strictly secret mind. Would you go to the guard house and ask if Wing Commander Allcock is back on camp. If he is, will you ask if he will come and see me on a very urgent matter. Don't mention my request to the rest of the staff. I am relying on you!"

So there I was standing in the guard house waiting to give my message to the orderly officer. Eventually, this very nice officer came in and said, "Tell Mona that Willie came back off leave last night and I will tell him right away." He winked at me when I turned to walk out and I blushed!

Now there's a turn-up for the books, 'Mona', she kept that one quiet! I chuckled to myself walking back about 'Willie Allcock'! I would love to share this info with the girls but I just can't – dammit.

Still no sign of Mark, seems as though he's just vanished.

Willie Winco or should I say 'Winki' came over to visit 'Glamour Puss' and asked me to direct him to her room as though he had never been there before. But on the other hand, I expect he preferred windows!

"How is she?" he asked.

"Well, Miss Harp ate a hearty breakfast," I replied.

"Jolly good show. What a trooper!" he said.

Chapter 13

This morning, on opening up the bar, to my surprise Mark strolled in and there he was in uniform and wearing slippers.

"For goodness sake, what are you doing Mark?" I asked, "go and get properly dressed or else you will get into trouble."

"Just listen to me for five minutes, Eve," he said, "and I'll explain to you why I am in slippers and why I stood you up. At the time in question I was in a place from where there was no escape."

"Alright, I'll listen," I said.

"Well, it was like this, I climbed the water tower in the field next to the camp because I wanted to paint the beautiful sunset. I had just mixed my paint, sitting on the rim of the water tower and I reached over to get my oil paper out of my satchel when, to my horror, I fell into the tank! The water level was very low and there was no way that I could climb out, so I just had to keep swimming and resting against the sides until the water level rose enough for me to heave myself up and climb out! I was in there for a day and a half and since getting back to camp I have been in the sick bay."

"Well, well," I said, "I have heard some excuses in my time but that one is a corker!"

"Believe me, Eve, it's the gospel truth, I can prove it." And with that he removed his slippers and showed me his feet that were indented and looked like orange peel, as did his arms and legs.

"Oh, I'm so sorry for disbelieving you," I said, "but why the slippers?"

"Because, my dear, my feet are incredibly sore and I am excused boots," he replied. "With a bit of luck, Eve, I will see you at the weekend for the sergeants, 'do', as I so want to have the first dance with you! But, now I've seen you to explain, I'm going back to my billet to sleep and sleep because all that unwanted exercise in that blasted tower has sapped my strength!"

Before he left he held my hands in his and said, "Goodnight, my dear girl, God bless and sweet dreams."

He touched my heart, and what a story and my god, one hell of a nightmare being trapped in that water.

Jean and Polly asked what Mark was talking so earnestly to me about.

"Oh nothing of any importance," I replied, thinking to myself it is best kept to myself. On a camp there is not much room for privacy or secrecy.

Miss Harp is still 'unwell' so has only been coming in for part of the day and as a consequence I have been run off my feet. I asked Lily, the lady from the village who comes in daily, to fill a large bath with chips. Polly filled it with water and then gave her the low-down on how to use the chipper.

"Then, when you have done that, Lily," I said, "put in a tiny piece of coal."

"Why coal?" she asked.

"Well, it's a well-known fact that it stops the chips from going brown," I said and picked up a small piece of coal to make sure she understood and placed it on the shelf. "I will leave it there and come back later to see how you are getting on."

I spent two very busy hours in the bar and was just thinking about going to check on Lily when Polly rushed in.

"Come quick, Eve. You are never going to believe this!" There was Lily standing by the bath with the empty coal bucket in her hand. The stupid woman had tipped a whole bucket of coal into the chips and it was a black disaster, including the chips! Lily's excuse was that she only did what I had told her to do. Give me strength, I thought!

When leaving, she asked me if it would be alright to come in the morning so I asked her to come in at 10.00 and clean out the billets. What could go wrong with that task, I thought. How wrong I was! She only left the tap on in the bathroom sink with the plug in and there was water streaming out into the corridor! 'Glamour Puss' was standing there with water lapping around her ankles, shouting at me, "Turn that bloody tap off and get the stupid cow off the camp!"

"I am sorry, Eve," said Lily weakly, "can I come back tomorrow?"

"I don't think that would be a good idea, Lily," I said.

"Ah well," she replied, "I was only trying to help!"

It took an age to sweep out the water and mop up and that is how Jean and I spent our afternoon off!

This morning Miss Harp is back on duty and looking at me from under hooded eyes asked, "What the hell was going on with that woman, where were you? You should have kept an eye on her."

I replied, "Miss Harp, we were very busy and I was up to my neck in paperwork in the office *and* on the bar, helping out as there was a new batch of recruits all waiting to be fed and watered. And," I added, "I do not have eyes in the back of my head!"

"Alright, Eve," she answered sharply, "I get the message, loud and clear. There's no need to be flippant!"

"It's so nice to see you've made a quick recovery, Miss Harp," I said, "and looking so well. The rest has done you good. I hope you will find everything in the office shipshape and Bristol fashion. It is so nice to have you back!"

With that said, through gritted teeth, I made a quick exit before I blew my top. She certainly is one hell of a mixed-up woman!

This afternoon I went for a walk with Jean and Polly, the snowdrops lay in clusters along the hedgerows and it was so nice to escape for a short time from the camp. I also wanted to see the water tower that Mark had so unfortunately fallen into. It was situated in the middle of a field quite isolated from the camp, so there would have been no use crying out for help.

He must have been crazy to climb up there!

"What's so interesting about that water tower?" asked Polly.

"Nothing," I replied, "I just wondered why it's been situated there."

Changing the subject, I said, "Come on, let's pick a posy of snowdrops to put in our room."

Miss Harp is back ensconced in her room. When I went in this morning to pick up the keys she looked as though she had been crying.

"Are you not feeling well again?" I asked.

"Just be a good girl and hold the fort for me today," she replied, "I am feeling so sad and depressed and if Wing Commander Allcock calls by tell him that I am receiving no one today." And with a sniff she said dramatically, "I just can't go on!"

"Shall I ask the MO to come over and see you?" I asked.

"No, not at all. He will be no use for what ails me," she replied accompanied by more sniffing.

I have now put two and two together and come up with 'man trouble' – in other words, 'Winco Willie' – I wonder what he has been up to!!

It was another day of being run off my feet but there was no way I was playing 'nursie' to a middle-aged lovesick woman this time, so I handed the role over to Esme, who was not best pleased. Everything was going well and I even had time to put my feet up with a cup of coffee when Esme rushed into the office trailing blood in her wake. She had badly cut her hand on one of the sharp knives in the kitchen. I quickly grabbed a large towel and some tea cloths from the cupboard and wrapped them around her injured hand, grabbed a scarf of Miss Harp's that was hanging on the back of a chair and put her arm up in a temporary sling. Doreen rang the Medical Officer and he said to bring her right over.

His surgery was so small that there was only room to stand and for one chair, and he was sitting on it. There was a young medical orderly standing by and poor Esme was shaking all over and was as white as a sheet so I asked the MO if there was a chair that she could sit on.

"Oh, this won't take long," he said examining Esme's gash. "Roll her sleeve up," he said to the orderly, "Just going to give you an injection, girlie, it won't hurt."

When Esme saw the needle coming towards her she panicked and wet herself!

It splashed all over the orderly's boots, up my legs and in my shoes and all over the surgery floor in a great puddle! The poor lad stood rooted to the spot with his mouth open!

"I am so sorry," I said to the MO.

"No need to say sorry, it often happens. It's shock," he said. He came round his desk and gave Esme his chair. And then to the boy, "Don't just stand there, Smith, jump to it, at the double, get a broom and mop and some Jeyes fluid from next door."

"Yessir, yessir!" standing to attention.

The MO put three stitches in Esme's hand, dressed the infection and put it back in the 'Miss Harp scarf' sling.

"Well done, jolly good show!" he said to me and we squelched our way slowly back to the NAAFI.

I put off relating the episode to Miss Harp, I'll leave it till the morning. I reasoned, I couldn't face having a backlash from her and with her current 'man troubles' her mood would not be pleasant. So, I put Esme to bed in the billet and then went back to pick up the reins in the bar. What a day.

Doreen whispered to me when I came into the kitchen, "The madam is in the office with the Romeo!" So, I ate breakfast then went back to the billet to check on my patient. Finding Esme much improved I continued my duties.

I was just beginning to re-stock the shelves of my bar when a beaming Miss Harp asked me how I was and would I like her to help me putting up the stock. I nearly fell through the floor – my, my, I thought, Wingco Willie must have come up trumps! It was then that I related to her, our trip to the MO but left out the rupture of Esme's waterworks.

"Poor girl," she said, "but you did the right thing, Eve. I am so pleased you are here. It's a great weight off my shoulders to know I have someone I can rely on."

Well, well I thought, how long will this nicey nicey bit last? What, I wonder, has she got planned for me?

Esme is back on duty today looking none the worse for wear and said to me, "I hope that medical orderly doesn't come in the canteen when I'm serving. How can I look him in the face after peeing on his boots!"

Miss Harp is still in a jovial mood so Willie Wingco must be dancing to her tune. Let's hope it lasts!

Last night we had a dress rehearsal and I've decided to wear my midnight-blue satin cocktail dress, which I bought from Bobbies when I was doing my modelling stint. Jean is wearing a black lace dress with red lining and I have lent her my red court shoes, and Esme offered her red clip-on earrings to complete the ensemble. So, only one more day to go until the officers' do and the air is charged with excitement.

Poor Polly was getting into quite a state of anxiety over what to wear and when she opened her wardrobe said, "What do you think I can wear out of this motley assortment?" and Esme replied, "I must say, there's not a lot to choose from!"

"Eve, you must help me," she said.

"Don't worry," I replied, "I'll see what I can come up with," although having made that promise I hadn't got a clue what to do. I am sure this lot think that I have a magic wand, even 'Glamour Puss' is on that list!

Today we had a delivery from the NAAFI bakery of tray upon tray of pastries and cakes, all destined for the officers' shindig.

After all the trials and tribulations of sorting out what to wear from our meagre wardrobes I just hope we have time to trip the light fantastic on the dance floor in all our finery. I had quite a problem kitting out Esme, but managed to borrow Miss Harp's old Singer sewing machine and with a bit of help from Jean, we transformed one of my dresses to fit her. We even sewed sequins around the bodice; the dress being black with red kick pleats, it needed something to shine. Esme is thrilled and Jean said to her, "Cinders, you WILL go to the Ball and with a bit of luck, nab a Prince!"

When we arrived at the hanger it was a hive of various RAF ranks setting up the buffet tables and Bar where large barrels of beer and crates of glasses were being stacked. The RAF band was tuning up on the makeshift stage but Madame Harp had given us strict orders that we were to stay behind the tables at all times while we were on duty, "Now do you understand, any skiving off is forbidden" she said, looking over at Polly, "have you got that?"

"Don't look at me like that, Miss!" Polly answered back.

"I know you, Polly."

"As if I would!" said Polly, smiling sublimely.

I was next to get my orders, "Eve, I leave you in charge. Keep your eye out at all times!"

I thought, how the hell am I going to do that and serve drinks at the bar. I wanted to answer back but let it pass.

We were rushed off our feet from the start and as the night wore on I had to ask for help especially with the bar, so was relieved when two young recruits came to help me out. Several of the arrogant 'moustache' brigade demanded, "Where's the head on this pint?" to which I was tempted to reply in no uncertain terms, but just smiled sweetly and said, "So sorry, sir, I will try and do better next time!"

In the meantime Glamour Puss was swanning around the officers. She never came over once to see if we were coping. So I was very pleased when Mark came in and asked, "Why are you behind the bar? You should be out on the dance floor."

I replied, "But Mark, we can't until Miss Harp gives her say-so."

"Just leave the old trout to me," he said, "Go on all of you, over to the billet and get your glad rags on!"

We did not need telling twice and hightailed it back to get ready for the shindig. When I returned Mark was waiting in the doorway and I could hear the band striking up a waltz. He held my hand and swept me onto the dance floor and I did not want that waltz to end, it was sheer magic. After we had danced a foxtrot Mark said to me, "I have to go now and take the old trout for a dance."

"But, why?" I asked.

"Because I promised her," he replied, "that's my penance for getting you girls off the hook!"

While he was away dancing with the old T., I was asked to dance by a very charming air gunner called Joe. The band had struck up a quickstep and he was one hell of a good dancer, and I had always shone at the quickstep so we really went for it! We took to the floor and before long we were in the centre of the room, jiving away completely unaware that we were on our own and that everyone else had moved back into a circle of spectators.

"Oh god," I said to Joe, "we're on our own!"

"Don't fret, girl, let's just go for it – it's a piece of cake."

But I could see, out of the corner of my eye, Glamour Puss giving me the evil eye.

"Oh hell, I'm for it now!" I said to Joe.

"You worry too much, she's just jealous, silly old bat! I've had a few run-ins with her," he said through gritted teeth, "She thinks she is god's gift to men! I would like to take you out sometime, pretty lady, if you will let me."

"But Joe, I am friendly with Mark McLean at the moment," I replied.

"Well if ever that comes to an end I'll be waiting in the wings. I'll just have to settle for having you in my dreams for now!" he said.

He was quite handsome in a rugged way, stocky build and a few inches taller than me, with dark hair and mischievous dark-brown eyes. Being in the NAAFI you have the opportunity to meet so many handsome and interesting young men as they come from all walks of life.

Mark came over to me for the next dance which was my favourite, the tango. It was the last dance of the night for me as we all had to start clearing up after that. The young lads were very good and had done the lion's share of the stacking of glasses into crates, so it was just a case of overseeing them dispatched back to the NAAFI. Mark came back to the canteen and helped and then we sat awhile in the kitchen and drank coffee and talked.

Polly and Jean were quite tipsy so entertained us doing the rumba around the room. Polly had piled fruit on her head saying she was Carmen Miranda, the Cuban actress. The grapes stuck fast to her head but the bananas went south!

Mark remarked, "You didn't tell me you could jive."

"Oh I learnt that during the war, from the Yanks when I was a Land girl," I replied.

"Do tell me more," he said.

"Nothing else to tell," I answered.

He looked at me, smiling and said, "I think you may be a dark horse and I'm going to get quite a few surprises."

"You can sure say that," piped up Polly, "after that quickstep that turned into a jive that bordered on a jitterbug. We didn't think she had it in her!"

We are meeting up again at the weekend as Mark has tickets for the opera, Madame Butterfly. That is, if 'Glamour Puss' doesn't put the kybosh on it – I am now sure that that woman has an evil streak in her.

It's my day off and I'm going into Bridgenorth to do some clothes shopping. That is, if there is anything worthwhile in the stores to buy. It is rather austere in the country at present and not much to choose from. However, we are all in the same boat and it will take a time to recover after the War. At least we all feel safer now it's over and can breathe more easily. In my teenage years I had to grow up very quickly when we were being bombed day and night. My schooling came to an abrupt end and there were many nights spent in air raid shelters which were damp and dreary and days when you never changed your clothes. I wanted so much to go on to further education as my dream was to be a teacher but all the college courses were cancelled.

Chapter 14

Today I was the only one in the kitchen. Miss Harp had employed a new cook called Lizzie, temporarily until Annie gets back off sick leave, and I had orders to show her the ropes before I opened up the bar. This scrawny looking woman screwed up her lips and said angrily, "What do *you* want?" I was, at the least, taken aback by this rudeness.

"I have come to help you find your way around," I said politely but with authority, "so would you be so good as to follow me and I will give you the low-down on where everything is."

"I certainly don't want any stuck-up madam telling me what to do. Now pass over those store keys and I'll weigh out my own ingredients," she replied tartly, and with that this odious woman ferreted around in her dirty apron pocket and produced a battered dog-end which she was about to light up!

"Stop right there," I said angrily, "how dare you smoke in our kitchen, around food! And another thing," by this time I was on a roll, "go into the linen cupboard and discard that filthy apron and get a clean one. And do it now, Lizzie, do you understand me loud and clear?"

"Oh, alright then," she replied, "no need to get arsey with me. I suppose you must be the chargehand!"

"Yes, that's right, that's me. Now follow me into the store and weigh up the ingredients you will need for the bar menu and the staff, and keep your lip to yourself." Oh hell, I thought, come back quick to the fold, Annie, before I am tempted to do something I will regret.

The opera 'Madam Butterfly' was fabulous. We were late coming out of the Theatre Royal so Mark hired a taxi back to camp. We entertained the driver when we sang one of the songs from the opera:
Oh tell me pretty Maiden are there any more at home like you
There are a few kind Sir... etc.
Whether it was to his liking I do not know, but anyhow he whistled along.

Glamour Puss is being very quiet – I wonder what she is brewing up for us, I dread to think!

On my next day off Mark and I went to Worcester. It was a lovely Spring day and we went for a trip up the river in the old pleasure steamboat. Mark was eager to take out a rowing boat but I declined because I usually end up having an argument with the oars, which never seem to go in the right direction. Afterwards we went to the Candena Café and it was yet again one of those lovely days to remember.

Today Lizzie was in the kitchen rolling out pastry. And there she was, puffing away on a cigarette, ash cascading over the pastry and there on the table was a cat!

Polly shouted over to her, "Where has that cat come from?"

"It's mine," she replied.

"Well, that's disgusting, Lizzie," I said angrily, "get that blasted cat out of here now and while you are at it, the ciggie as well. That pastry can go straight in the bin and you can scrub that table down."

"My, my, Miss Uppity, we are in a bad mood today," she retorted sarcastically.

"Bad mood," I replied, "you haven't seen anything yet. How dare you. Have you never heard the words hygiene or cleanliness? It's no good, Lizzie, I will have to report you. We can't go on like this, the troops could end up with food poisoning."

"So could we!" piped up Polly.

"Oh alright," she said, "I'll take Tiddles to the billet."

"Make sure you shut your door when you do," said Polly, "I don't want that cat peeing on my bed!"

When Miss Harp was settled in the office I took her in a mug of coffee. "What can I do for you?" she asked.

"It's about Lizzie," I said.

After going through the whole episode of the cat, smoking, ash, dirty aprons etc. she turned around in her chair and said, "You deal with it. Can't you see I'm busy with this bloody accounts book."

"Could we not get another cook?" I asked.

"Bloody hell, no. You sort it or if not you will find yourself doing the cooking. I just don't have time for all this 'argy bargy'!"

I stormed out, giving the office door an almighty bang as I left. There was no sign of Lizzie but lo and behold, Pussy was large as life sitting on the kitchen table scratching away at its fur. To say I was fuming is the understatement of the year. I picked Pussy up by the scruff of its neck and dropped it out of the window. In my stressed condition I had forgotten that we were on stilts, and to my horror heard this shriek from below. On looking down I could see that pussy had landed on an airman's head, who just happened to be passing by at the time!

"I am so sorry," I called down. He laughed, "I was told by my mum that it rained cats and dogs," he said, "but I sure as hell never believed her, honey!"

He was from Newfoundland I learnt later.

"Come up into the kitchen," I called down.

"Shall I bring the moggie?"

"NO!" I almost screamed. I left Polly to look after him and made sure she gave him coffee and biscuits.

"What about Miss Harp?" she asked.

"Oh, her," I replied, "she's busy in the office, up to her neck in paperwork and doesn't want to be disturbed."

Mark is coming back later and I can't wait to escape from this madhouse. At present he is my only reason for staying on here. Until my time is up he is the only bright light on the horizon. Working with Miss Harp is like treading on eggshells every day and now I have this odious woman, Lizzie to deal with and the flea-ridden cat which should never have been allowed onto the premises.

Mark and I went for a walk by the river this afternoon and it was lovely to be away from the camp and out in the fresh air. It was a lovely Spring day, there were clumps of primroses along the hedgerows, and so peaceful. Everything was fresh and coming to life with the pink blossom on the hawthorn. We sat on a bench watching the river run by and the beautiful swans gliding elegantly along. Mark started telling me about his War years when he went on many mission over Germany in a Lancaster bomber. He told of all the many close mates that he had lost at that time that never came back and that he still had great sadness in his heart for them. A solitary tear trickled down his face.

"Mark," I said, "please don't tell me any more if it upsets you so much."

"But I want to tell you. Eve, I feel at ease with you, you are so calm and compassionate and a good listener and also I feel I can open up to you and I have never felt like that with anyone else. That is, of course, if you don't mind me burdening you with my stories."

"Not at all, you go ahead and I will sit here quietly and listen." I held his hand and the stories began. I was blown away by his bravery and felt honoured that he had chosen me to talk to.

Mark's Story

Mark told me an amazing true story about the time he spent in France as an agent during the early part of the War. He went on to say that as he spoke French and German fluently and as he was also blond and blue-eyed, he fitted the bill perfectly when he volunteered his services to be an agent.

Apparently, when he was a teenager in Scotland, to earn pocket money he would go along and help the local barber. He soon became an accomplished hairdresser and enjoyed the experience and especially conversing with the clients. Mark said that they certainly let their hair down and divulged some of their deepest secrets. This experience came in very useful, he remarked, when he was given the job as barber for the officers at a German barracks in France.

I was transfixed by how this story was unfolding. He went on to say that they were parachuted into France and on landing they were quickly taken to 'safe houses' by the Resistance. They were then issued with the necessary papers and he met his co-worker who was called Marie. She played the part of radio transmitter, sending out valuable information to Britain which Mark had passed on from what he picked up from the careless conversation of the SS officers after they had indulged in too many Schnapps.

I interrupted him at this stage and asked, "Were you not scared to death that every day they would find you out?"

His answer was, "Not at all at that time, it gave me a buzz to think I was getting one over on the bastards! My thoughts and concern was for Marie. She was, after all, out in the open to all dangerous situations." He went on to say that he made friends with a couple of SS officers who invited him to their mess and, "I was feeling very pleased with myself at playing the part. I just got carried away and bloody well drank too much, so ended up being frogmarched out of the mess on the way to Gestapo headquarters to be questioned."

"Well," I said, "what did you say?"

"Eve, you asked what I said, well, I was asked a simple question by one of the elderly officers there, 'what the time was?' and how did I reply – in English, 11.30!!!

"Firstly," Mark said, "they gave me the softly, softly approach but when the bastards realised I was not going to talk then things began to get nasty. Firstly, I was swiped across the back of the head which sent me flying across the room. Then I was hauled up by the hair to face this thick-set evil, cold bastard who slammed me back into the chair with such force it made my teeth rattle. Then the real torture began.

"I was told to strip to my underpants and they proceeded to grind out lighted cigarettes into my body, the backs and palms of my hands and the soles of my feet and then to pull out my toenails. By this time I couldn't take much more, but had to think of a plan to play for time. So I looked up at the evil bastards and said that I would talk, but first can I please go to the lavatory or my bowels will erupt. To my utter amazement they agreed and beckoned to a young guard on the door to escort me. I was taken down this long corridor and then down to the bowels of the building. I was shuffling along on my agonising feet. 'Hurry,' I pleaded to him, clutching my stomach in agony. He pushed the door of a lavatory open and barked, 'Be quick, this is a staff lavatory, and don't lock the door.'

"But I did," Mark said, "I quietly slid the bolt across and then looked around for an escape route. There above the ancient cistern, was a small window, partly open but alas very high up." But, Mark said, he just had to try, so he hauled himself up on to the antiquated cistern praying it did not come away from the wall. Balancing on the top he gradually pulled himself up to the narrow window ledge, then with one almighty push managed to push the window outwards. But getting his frame through the narrow gap was the bugbear, but thank god, he said, he was of slight build but he had grave doubts about getting his shoulders through. He managed his head and neck, so summoned every ounce of strength and turned his body, and with a tight squeeze on his side he slid through to the ground and was free.

"And I ran like hell through the streets which were icy cold with frost, but my sore feet were thankfully numbed by the extreme cold. I dodged down alleyways and hid in doorways at any sign of the Bosch, and eventually reached the countryside and by sheer luck came upon a stream of refugees who were making their way to the mountains in a bid to escape into Spain." But, they warned him that the journey would be treacherous, not only from the appalling weather conditions, but also having to dodge the German patrols. But what choice had they got? "So, we began the journey through the mountains, which was horrendous, and all I am going to say now at this point into my story is that so many good people died on that journey.

"We huddled together at night to keep warm and I was given a pair of boots that belonged to one of the unfortunate walkers, but without those gallant, courageous, lovely people to whom I owe my life, I would not be here today telling you my story. You asked, Eve, if we reached Spain and freedom, and yes, we did but at a cost. God bless them all. Just to say that when I was awarded my medal of honour, I still to this day do not feel I deserved it. It should have been them not me, for their fearless courage. Without them I would have died."

Mark told me that of every hundred men recruited to fly with Bomber Command during the War, more than half died. The level of sacrifice was appalling and it had been a hell of searchlights and guns. German night-fighters fired lethal bursts of gunfire into our British bombers so suddenly that the crews did not recover.

"These airmen were all so young and innocent and we were all so very close as aircrew, closer even than our own families, at that time. That's why it was so heartbreaking when anyone 'bought it'. We all had mascots, Eve, I had this small St Christopher medallion and thank god, it kept me safe. So open your hand because I am giving it to you for being such a good listener. To have found someone like you, who cares and who I feel so at ease with and peaceful – you see, my dear, I have so many demons I can't seem to get rid of… I would also like you to take care of my medals." (These were the DFC and DSO.)

"Are you sure, Mark?" I asked.

"Yes, yes I trust you."

On returning to the billet I locked everything away in my metal wardrobe for safe keeping.

This morning Mark went AWOL again and this time he was away for fourteen days. Apparently it was general knowledge with some of the recruits that he had a drink problem and went off on binges, to god knows where. I think that was probably why he had given me his medals for safe keeping. I realise now, when he mentioned to me about his demons that he was no doubt a very sick man mentally. I should think this was brought on by the suffering he had endured at the hands of the Gestapo and the continual bombing campaigns during the War. He was a very brave man and one of the young victims of that terrible war.

The day he opened his heart to me of his past, I went back to the billet and wept for him and thought I would flood the bathroom with my tears.

Polly was so concerned about me she called out, "Tell me what's wrong, Eve, is it old Harpie?"

"No, no it's nothing at all, I just have a cold," I sniffed, "and one hell of a headache."

I felt so utterly helpless. He just had this one mass of problems and when I suggested that he went for counselling he said, "They have tried but I'm afraid I'm going to occasionally go and drown my sorrows. But with you by my side, it will help."

I have grave doubts about that. I feel I wouldn't be strong enough emotionally to be there for him and his demons. So, I think it is a blessing I will be leaving here soon. I am very fond of him and will continue to be his friend while I am here. I just don't want my heart to rule my head and can't at the moment see any light at the end of that particular tunnel.

Chapter 15

Another busy day with the young recruits queuing up to get served, anxiously waiting to get to the bar. The queue stretched right outside, the full length of the canteen.

"No pushing and shoving. You will get served more quickly if you form an orderly queue," I said to them.

Polly helped me by giving them their purchases while I took the money. They then dashed down to the other bar for mugs of tea and a 'wad', something like bread pudding only more solid. The canteen was packed to the rafters for a while until the orderly corporal came along shouting, "On the double, lads, tea break over, back to billets!"

The place cleared fairly quickly with only a few stragglers left and it was great to relax a bit until the next time around. Polly and I filled the empty shelves with boot polish, Blanco, Brasso, dusters and ciggies which had sold so well today. Their next port of call was the barber, so when they come in tomorrow they will be minus a lot of hair! They are very young, fresh-faced and a picture of innocence.

Lizzie did not turn up for breakfast duty, so I ended up doing it for the staff myself. After they had made short work of my bacon, eggs, tomatoes and toast they were only going to slope off back to the billet!

"Oh no you don't," I said, calling them back, "there is the small matter of washing up the dishes and frying pan. And who is brave enough to take over Miss Harp's breakfast?"

"I'll take it," volunteered Jean, "and shall I tell her about Lizzie?"

"No, you can leave out that info, in the meantime I'll go and see what ails Lizzie. With a bit of luck she will have gone AWOL with pussy!"

Mark came back to camp today, looking decidedly the worse for wear. He asked me if I had missed him and I replied that if I had known where he was then perhaps I may have been worried.

"Now you are talking in riddles, Eve. I'll explain later, when I'm off duty," he said. Do I really want to know?

This morning I asked Old Harpie if it would be alright to put Mark's medals in the office safe for safe keeping as I was on edge about keeping them in the billet.

The look on her face was of shock horror, "What the hell are you doing with his medals?" she asked angrily.

"Well, if you must know, Miss Harp, Mark asked me to look after them for him."

"Why you, why didn't he ask me?"

"We are friends and he trusts me," I answered.

"You are are you, since when? You kept that a secret, Madam!"

"Well, put it this way," I said as calmly as I could, "I am entitled to have a boyfriend in my free time, or do I have to ask your permission or seek your approval?"

With that, she slammed the door on the safe with such force that it rattled.

"When you next see him," she said icily, "tell him to come and see me."

Oh god, I thought, I have well and truly cooked my goose now. She really fancies him and I can see trouble ahead! What a nasty piece of work she is, maybe I should remind her of Romeo 'Wingco' falling out of her bedroom window! I think I'll save that one for when I leave! This afternoon Mark is going to paint my portrait and I certainly don't want Harpie to know about that!

It was one of those lovely days, spring sunshine and just a gentle breeze. Mark had me sitting on a bench by the riverside while he settled at his easel.

I kept asking if I could move as I had cramp in my leg, "Not yet, I'll let you know when you can move," he said.

Why the hell did I agree to this posing torture, I wondered, I know now what models have to endure or perhaps they don't get cramp.

"What a fidget you are!" said Mark. I pleaded with him and told him I was in agony.

"Just another ten minutes," he said, "think of something nice, like sea crashing against the rocks!"

His ten minutes went on and on for thirty minutes by which time I had endured enough and rose from the bench, "It's no good, Mark. You can think of sea crashing on rocks if you like, but I've had enough and I'm going back to camp."

"Wait, wait for me," he shouted after me, "come back!"

Like hell, I thought, I felt like telling him where to stick his paintbrushes!

Lazy Lizzie is back on duty with a face like a wet weekend, no pussy though!

Mark sent me a letter via one of the recruits. It said, 'Sorry, can we try again? Eve, you are more fiery than I thought, hiding behind that calm exterior. I must confess it took me by surprise but you are a lovely lady and I will be in the canteen tomorrow so will see you then, my love.'

Harpie decided to take over preparing and cooking the staff dinner which took us all by surprise. She said, in her haughty manner, "It will be fish and chips."

"I don't eat fish!" piped up Polly.

"You jolly well will, you fussy madam, so there!" she retorted.

Last night Mark came over with my portrait. It really was lovely.

"Thank you, Mark, it really is a remarkable likeness of me. How did you manage to finish it because if you remember, I bailed out on you that day?"

"That was easy," he replied, "because I have a mirror image of your beautiful face!" I blushed with embarrassment.

"Will you be kind enough to keep it for me," I asked, "as there is no place in the billet to put it."

"No problem at all," he replied, "I will hang it in the classroom at the Education centre and then my young recruits can view it when they come in."

Oh lordy, I thought, I do not really want anyone else to see it, but hopefully they won't recognise me.

"Please don't tell them it's me," I asked him.

"For god's sake, Evie, why not? You are lovely!"

"Please don't."

"Alright, I'll just ask them who they think it is," he laughed.

"No, no not that either!"

"Just teasing, my, you look even more lovely when you're angry – your eyes flash!"

What a charmer he is.

Last night several of the girls felt unwell and I felt yucky. Polly was in bed, too exhausted to go on duty, having spent most of last night in the bathroom. We had all complained at the time when Harpie sat with us at the dinner table dishing up the fish and chips she had cooked. I took one bite of the fish and it tasted horrible with the tang of being rotten.

"I can't eat this," I said, "it's off."

Polly joined in, "I can't either."

"Well, it tastes perfectly alright to me," Harpie proclaimed, rolling the jar of tomato sauce and bottle of vinegar down the table at us, "put some of that on it!"

Lizzie was wolfing it down, so was Esme. Perhaps it is me, I thought, so as not to cause any more aggro, I shook out a substantial dollop of tomato sauce over it and swallowed a piece down followed by a few chips. Then I left the table, throwing the remains of the revolting fish and chips into the pig swill bin, with Harpie staring at me fiercely but not saying a word.

For the last five days I have been off sick. The first day I was so ill with a high temperature and excruciating stomach pains that Harpie had to send for the local doctor. Polly later told me that she had been very reluctant to do so. She was an absolute pain in the neck and kept coming over insisting that I eat something, which was the last thing I wanted. I felt so ill and was not improving so the doctor had me transferred to the local hospital where after several tests the verdict was fish poisoning. I came back after four days, a whole stone lighter. The doctor who had looked after me reported old Harpie to the health authority, so my name was mud in her eyes. He also signed me off for two weeks to convalesce and advised me to get well away from there and from Miss Harp's bullying tactics. He said that she is an evil woman and that from the conversation he had had with her he thought her mentally unbalanced and that she should never be in charge of young women. Then he laughed and added, "Also man-mad! That disgusting woman even came on to me, but all she got was the sharp end of my tongue!"

Mark was pleased to see me well again but was sad that I was leaving. So I just said goodbye to all the staff and Mark promised to write and to come and see me. I just wanted to get away from that place and never set foot in it again.

Chapter 16

I spent a lovely two weeks at home. My family wanted me to stay longer but I wanted to get back to Newton Abbot and all my lovely friends and Miss Kitty, not forgetting the Devonshire countryside and the sea air. My weight had plummeted to 7st 12lbs but it is great to feel well again after that painful ordeal. I just hope that harridan gets her comeuppance one day!

Today, thank god, I am back at Denbury. Miss Kitty is furious about Harpie and Mr Hawksworth, the district manager, is coming by tomorrow to see me about what is going on there. Miss Kitty was most concerned about my weight loss, "Just look at you, Eve, are you sure you are well enough to work?"

"Oh yes, Miss Kitty," I assured her, "I am. In fact it's much better for me to keep busy."

"Well, promise me you won't overdo it," she said adding, "We are all very fond of you here and missed you like hell while you were away. So take it slowly." Looking at me she said, "We'll soon put some meat on those bones!"

I felt like I wanted to weep, not from sadness but joy. All the girls, including 'woe is me Vera', hugged me and I had that lovely feeling of belonging and coming home.

It took me by surprise to see that Vera was still there as she was supposed to have been posted abroad. I will have to ask her later about that. Marge is still away on leave and Diana, well what can I say about Diana except that she is head over heels again, this time a sergeant on the camp called Simon. Nancy has a certain sadness about her and is very quiet which puzzles me and I asked Diana if she was alright.

"Oh Nancy is Nancy, she is just back off leave so I expect it is being back here, Eve."

Today I received a lovely letter from Mark. He said that the 'old trout' had got the push, 'so come back to the fold, I miss you so. The light has gone out of my life and it's not the same going into the canteen and not seeing your smiling face!' He said, it wasn't just him that felt that way but many of the recruits too. I must write back and tell him that I am much happier here and there is no going back but that should not stop us from being friends!!

Today I encountered a lot of new faces in the canteen eager to get served on their lunch break. One young lad asked me if I would write a letter to his mum for him and when I asked him why he couldn't write his own letter he whispered, "I can't write very well."

"Are you having me on, young man?" I asked.

"No, no," he blushed to the roots of his hair, "I just can't!"

"Well alright then, but are you sure there is no one else that could help you?"

"No one, honest. Please, Miss!"

I asked him what his name was and what he wanted me to write. "It's Timmy," he said and, "just say, 'Dear mum, I am well and happy. I have been on the firing range and Sarge was very pleased with me and I hit a bullseye. I hope to get leave when the six weeks training is up. Love to little Maisie and give my little dog Jack a cuddle for me. Tell dad I am keeping a stiff upper lip. Thank Nan and Gramps for the money, it will help no end. We are not far from the sea here. Love from Timmy. (SWALK)'"

"Do you know what you are doing, Eve?" asked Diana, "you will end up having every Tom, Dick and Harry queuing up for you to write their letters!"

"No, I won't this is just a one-off," I replied. She walked off laughing saying, "Do you want to bet?"

Another day, another dollar and yet another letter from Mark saying that he is planning to come down here next weekend. Well, I doubt that very much, knowing his track record with his binges. It is sad but he is so mixed up trying to deal with his demons and as I've said before I don't feel strong enough to deal with all that. I also had a card from Marge and she is back at the weekend and we both have a lot of catching up to do. It's my day off today and the girls brought me over breakfast in bed with a note from Miss Kitty to, 'have a good rest' – a bit different from Bridgenorth!

Yesterday afternoon we all went to the cinema on camp where they were showing Fred Astaire and Ginger Roberts in 'Top Hat'. I had seen it before but we all strolled in armed with bags of popcorn and it was just like old times.

This morning, Marge came back off leave. She looked different as she's had her hair cut really short which gives her a pixie look. I told her that I thought it suited her and she said, "I hate it, I wish I had never had it cut. Donnie was scissor-happy and poncing around saying, 'Leave it to me, dearie, you will go out of my salon a new girl!'"

"But, Marge," I said, "it is lovely! It emphasises your cheekbones, and with those lovely dangly green earrings you are wearing you look absolutely stunning. So get out there on the bar and blow away all those new recruits!"

Today I was asked by a young recruit called Joe to write him a love letter to his girl. "Please, Miss, I will be ever so grateful if you would," he said, grinning from ear to ear.

"I suppose you've got this information about me on the grapevine?" I said.

"Well, yes," he answered, shifting nervously from one foot to the other.

"Why can't you write to her yourself?" I asked.

"But, I don't really know how to go about it," he answered, "Please, Miss!"

So, here I go again, I thought, I've really let myself in for it. Her name was Rosie and he said that he would come in for it tomorrow and I said to him jokingly, "It will cost you!" He gave me the gist of what he wanted to say and I wrote:

'My darling Rosie, you are the light of my life, I love you so much my heart fills with joy every time we meet. I will be home on leave in two weeks' time and then, my darling, I can hold you in my arms and kiss your velvet lips. We all went on the range today for target practice and the corp. said that I was pretty hopeless and to go and get my eyes tested! But then, my love, perhaps they may excuse me on that score as I do not want to go and fight in Korea and the thought of it fills me with dread. Perhaps, and it is only perhaps, they will say that I am not suitable owing to the fact that I can't shoot straight, then I can come home to you. Say a prayer for me, darling. With love and kisses from your devoted boyfriend, Joe.'

Personally, having written that for the poor lad I thought, he hasn't got a hope in hell of getting out of it or escaping back home.

Later Diana remarked, "What did I tell you, Eve! You will now be in great demand for writing those love letters!"

"Yes, I know, Diana," I answered, "I don't suppose I could ask you to help me out now and again?"

"Well, put it this way," she replied, "I ain't no good at that sort of thing so ask Marge when she gets back!"

This morning, Nancy was not very well so Diana and I had the great pleasure of cleaning out the flues in the kitchen and lighting the fires of the cooking range ready for the cooks when they came on duty. At least there was no wind today so we didn't get a backlash of soot. Today was all quiet on the home front and no requests for letters, apart from one incident when one of the young recruits came into the canteen with tears streaming down his cheeks.

"What's wrong?" I asked him.

"I'm in deep trouble," he sobbed.

"Tell me about it," I said.

Through more breathless sobs, he stuttered, "I have lost all my kit!"

"But how? Someone has pinched it or is playing games with you. Come on now, dry your eyes, it may turn up. Some of the lads are playing a cruel joke on you," I said.

He looked up at me his eyes welling up with tears, "But I'll end up in the glasshouse when the sarge finds out," he wailed.

"Just wait there a while," I said, concerned, "Maybe I can help."

I went into the office to Miss Kitty and on relaying the sorry tale she said, "Eve, you must understand we are not running a welfare society here. You really have got to toughen up! But, just this once I will try to help although it may not do any good. Send the lad round to me and I will contact Henry. Just go back on the bar and serve the troops."

Later on it transpired the young lad's dilemma had been solved. Apparently three jokers from his billet had hidden the poor lad's kit.

Miss Kitty warned me again, "Please Eve, do not get involved again. You are not his auntie. You are just here to serve the troops. That's what the NAAFI is all about, we are here to serve. So no more stepping over that line. Of course," she added, "by all means commiserate with them when they come to you with their sad stories but just leave it at that. And Eve, what is all this that I have been hearing about you concerning letter writing?" She shook her head and remarked, "Are you sure you are in the right job, with all your 'talents'?"

"Well, Miss Kitty, it is just a one-off," I replied.

"Is it?" she asked, smiling, "Just whatever you do, do not let it get out of hand!"

Last night 'woe is me' Vera told me why she had passed up the chance for her posting overseas. "Because," she said, "I have fallen in love and his name is – and don't you dare laugh, Eve – Tarquin."

"Oh, that's a lovely name, Vera," I replied, "Where did you meet him?"

"Not here on camp," she replied, "but when you were away I went on a jolly with Ruby to Torquay and met him on the beach. Would you like to meet him?"

"Yes, I would, Vera," I replied, "it's very nice of you to ask me."

"By the way, Eve, could I borrow your short navy jacket with the velvet collar?" she asked.

"Yes, you may, Vera," I replied, "but do you think it will fit you?"

"Oh, it does," she said, "I tried it on, I hope you don't mind!"

God, I thought, is nothing sacred around here? Then I had another thought, how the hell did she get into my wardrobe without the key? I shall have to investigate that one. She had really taken me by surprise with her unusual request.

Miss Kitty asked me today if I would accompany her to the theatre in Exeter to see the ballet 'Sylvia'.

"How are we going to travel?" I asked.

"Oh, don't worry, Eve, it won't be like last time in the army lorry," she said, "We will take my Austin 7. It's about time 'old Milly' had a run out!"

"Oh will we?" I said querulously.

"Well, you don't sound very enthusiastic, girl, don't you want to accept my offer?" she asked.

"Oh yes, I do," I lied, "It will be great!" I was thinking, I hope she doesn't ask me to crank up the old jalopy. I had visions of us chugging our way to Exeter in clouds of smoke and loud bangs from the ancient exhaust.

"Henry is going to give it a good look over before we go," she said, reading my mind, "So don't fret, girl, everything will be dandy. Oh, before you go, Eve, what's wrong with Diana of late? She is very quiet, I hope she's not up to anything!"

"She's fine," I answered, "perhaps she's in love again, Miss Kitty!"

Diana's quiet period ended that night when she fell in through the billet window at midnight. Marge and Ruby had sewn up the arms and legs of her pyjamas as a joke and the air was blue as she threatened to tip us all out of our beds. But she was swaying all over the place, so fortunately was unable to carry out her threats. Marge and I managed to get her into bed and she lay there snoring her head off. At last, we have got 'madcap' Diana back, I must say the quietness was quite unnerving.

We have a new bunch of recruits on camp, mostly back from the Far East, so the queues were endless in the canteen. As fast as we filled the shelves on my net bar we were filling them up again with cigarettes, Blanco, dusters, boot polish, chocolate, writing pads and envelopes. The cooks were also run off their feet, dishing out mouth-watering meat pies and cakes of all description. My favourite were Eccles cakes, and each time I hoped to sample one on my lunch break Joan would say, "Sorry, Eve, they are all gone. Make sure you don't lose out tomorrow!" That's the story of my life – so near yet so far!

Last night I met Vera's boyfriend, Tarquin. My, he is handsome in a 'pretty boy' way, tall in stature with black, curly cropped hair and piercing blue eyes that seem to bore into you, which I found quite unnerving. While Vera was occupied elsewhere, he bent over and whispered in my ear, "Where have *you* been all my life?" I was so embarrassed. Oh hell, I thought, poor Vera, he is a creep.

Miss Kitty said, when I went into the office this morning to pick up the floats, "What the hell is that girl doing with a poser like that? When there are so many more real men on camp, I'll bet my bottom dollar he's a 'pansy' or so mixed up he doesn't know which side he's batting! Where the hell did she meet him?"

"In Torquay, on the beach," I replied.

"Well," she said, "my advice to her is to take him back there quick!"

Today, Nancy was back on duty but I still think that there is something troubling her as she looks so sad. But, when we ask her the answer is always the same, that she is fine. We have all made a point of filling the coal buckets for her and taking them into the kitchen. The blasted things are so heavy I honestly don't know how she manages to carry them up the steps, you need muscles like 'Popeye'."

This morning, Diana and I had the job of cleaning the tea urns. Miss Kitty is a stickler for keeping the urns shiny bright so that you are able to see your face in them. For this task we used salt and vinegar mixed together into a paste which was then rubbed into the copper of the urns with a great deal of elbow grease. When I first helped out on this task I was a real doubting Thomas thinking this will never work, but lo and behold they came up sparkling, shining like new and well worth the effort. So there's another tip to my bow!

Vera announced at breakfast this morning that Tarquin had asked her if there was any chance of him meeting up with any of the lovely, brave recruits on camp. Diana nearly choked on her toast and Miss Kitty looked under her eyelids at Vera, banged her empty coffee cup on the table and said to her, "Are you out of your mind, you stupid girl, can't you see what he is up to? He is dammed well using you!"

Vera replied, "He is in love with me!"

"Poppycock!" said Miss Kitty, "For god's sake, one of you tell her!"

When she said that, she looked over at me, "Well, I don't know what you want me to say," I muttered.

With that, Miss Kitty pushed back her chair saying, "Give me strength!" and then stormed off into her office.

Diana looked over at Vera and said, "He's one of them!"

"What do you mean?" asked Vera weakly.

"You know," replied Diana, "one of the limp-wrist brigade!"

I left the table, while Vera stared vacantly at Diana, and Marge followed in my wake saying, "She will get the message eventually."

"Not from me though," I replied, "In any case, there is no way he will be allowed on camp. He is a civilian and I am in no doubt Miss Kitty will stick her oar in with help from 'Sarge Henry'!"

Yet another surprise at the NAAFI! Whilst helping Nancy with the coal buckets this morning she asked, "Can you keep a secret, Eve?"

"Yes, of course I will, what is it?" I replied.

"I have a boyfriend and we're getting engaged!" she said.

"My word, Nancy, you have kept that one close to your chest. Who is he?"

"His name is Ernie and he's a corporal on the camp. I've been going out with him for two months," she said.

"I am so pleased for you, Nancy, I really am," I answered, "When's the wedding?"

"Not yet, Eve, we're saving up," she said.

"Would you like me to have a whip-round to buy you both an engagement present?" I offered.

"Oh no, not yet," Nancy said, "Perhaps next month. Then I'll tell everyone."

"Let me know when you're ready, Nancy, in the meantime it's our secret!"

Vera was rolling out pastry in the kitchen as I passed by to go to my bar when she tugged at the sleeve of my overall and said, "I want a word with you."

"Not now, Vera," I answered, "I'm just going to fill the shelves on my net bar."

"Well, later then!" she threatened, "what the hell is the matter with you lot? Nobody wants to discuss anything with me. I don't care what you bloody lot think, I love him and that's that. So stick that up your pipe and smoke it!"

Oh hell, poor Vera is in a great strop, I hope Miss Kitty can sort this one out and not leave it to me.

Diana's love life is back on track and 'Roger the dodger' is back in favour!

Nothing fails to amaze me here, Ruby has put in for a posting to Germany and when Margie asked her if it was a joke, Ruby replied, "No, not at all, I want to travel!"

"Well, you'll certainly do that, our Rube!" replied Marge.

A new batch of recruits came in today, quite a number returning from Malaya and Singapore, among them many regular soldiers. I have yet another new admirer. Apparently, he is the butcher on the camp named Bill, so the recruits informed me. They told me, "Butch fancies you no end!"

"Well, he can jolly well go and admire someone else, I am not interested!" I retorted.

This afternoon we spent a lovely time with Ruby's gran. She was disappointed at not seeing Diana and so was Roger, who asked me on the way back to camp if I knew what was wrong with Diana and also if I knew what was so important about the appointment in town. Poor chap, he was so upset. I just answered truthfully that I was in the dark about it too, "Roger," I said, "you must ask her yourself, after all it may be all above board and you are worrying about nothing."

"I hope you are right, Eve," he replied, "because I do love her so!"

Chapter 17

'Romeo Bill' was the first person in my queue this morning at break time. He is quite a gentleman, full of charm, very handsome with twinkling blue eyes. The recruits are asking me if he is now my boyfriend and my answer is, "NO, definitely not!" Bill just smiles and is back again day after day. One time I asked him if he had nothing better to do than stand at my bar.

"Well, no," was his answer, "I like looking at you. You are so lovely, Eve and I am hoping that one day you will let me take you on a date!"

I am secretly admiring him… he is so funny and makes me laugh and always seems to brighten up the day. But, deep down I am very unsure about accepting a date with him. Marge said, "Give him a chance, for heaven's sake, Eve, it's only a date! You take life far too seriously, go for it, go and have some fun!"

We received some very bad news today, Archie is dead. He was run over by a lorry in Berlin as he was crossing the road. Alice is in a state of shock and is, at present, staying with her sister in Liverpool. Dear Alice, I feel for her, such a short time ago we were preparing for her wedding. Oh hell, life is so hard. At times like this it makes you feel so helpless for there is nothing that one can do to ease the pain and torment. We all went to the village church this afternoon and sat alone and prayed for her. Dear, dear Alice, she and Archie had so many plans for the future. They were such a sweet couple and so much in love.

Miss Kitty shed a solitary tear when we told her. It ran down her cheek and as she wiped it away she said, "Get the brandy out of my cupboard, I am in need of it! My god, that poor girl, life is so cruel! Close the door on your way out, I want to be alone with my thoughts for a while."

Then it struck me that we really were like family to her. To explain it better, it feels warm and caring, a sense of belonging, that when the chips are down there is someone there to care and support you. Where else would you experience that in a work force apart from your own family? It is, as she is always saying, we are a team. We were all in sombre mood when we opened last night and glad when the shift was over.

Bill was in again today but this time with a different request. He said, "How about if, later on, I bring some rump steaks round to the kitchen and then the cook could put on some chips and we could all have a steak and chip supper. Now, does that sound like a good idea?" he asked with a smile.

"Well, no I don't think it is a good idea!" I replied.

Ruby was listening in on this conversation while she was restocking my shelves and interjected, "Oh Eve, don't be mean, let him come round tonight. My mouth is watering already just at the thought of my teeth getting around a rump steak! I can't remember the last time I even saw one!"

"Oh alright," I said to him, "you can come, but don't get any ideas!"

"No, of course not," he replied, grinning from ear to ear.

Miss Kitty was delighted when I asked her permission for Bill to bring our steak supper around.

"Of course, Evie, he's welcome anytime," she said, "and I look forward to meeting your young man."

"But, he is not my young man yet," I replied.

She smiled, "Ah, my dear girl, he will be. You mark my words!"

Bill arrived with the rump steak rolled up in his tunic jacket and Joan and Vera welcomed him as though he was the prodigal son.

Miss Kitty went to the bar and gave him a beer, "Come on, Eve, up the table and sit next to your young man," she said, winking mischievously at me.

The only one missing from the table was Nancy and she was under the weather again. Bill said to Joan, "Save a portion for her then she can have it later when she feels better."

I looked over and said, "That is kind of you, Bill," and he squeezed my hand under the table. "Not at all!" he said, smiling. I blushed when his hand touched mine and it was as though an electric shock passed through my body! This can't be happening, I thought. A few weeks ago he really irritated me, standing endlessly at my bar and now, like a bolt out of the blue, I have these feelings for him!

We are meeting up tomorrow, my day off, and he is taking me to the Races at Newton Abbot. I hope I back the winning horse.

Diana is still in a very quiet mood, not like her at all and she clams up every time one of us asks her what is wrong.

Bill and I had a lovely day at the Races. Bill's horse, 'Charmer' came in third and my horse alas is still running! Afterwards we went into town to a restaurant for dinner and Bill told me he had not long returned from the Far East. He had spent three years in Malaya and Singapore and lastly Tokyo and it was on the cards for him to go to Korea, "But," he said, "I am going to see if I can wangle a way out of that one!" I certainly hope so! I feel like I have known him all my life. Hell, I think I am falling in love – for real this time!

The steaks kept coming twice a week for all our suppers! Bill just fits in with all of us. It's uncanny, he is always on hand to help out when he is not on duty. If something goes wrong with the iron or a kettle etc. they say "Bill will fix it." In other words he is becoming a fixture and he is lovely! I cringe when I think back to when I was so curt and unkind to him. When we first started going out I said to him, "I'm sorry I was so mean to you."

"No problem," was his reply, "Faint heart never won fair maiden!"

Joan asked Bill what was his favourite pudding and he said that he was very partial to apple pie, so every so often we now have steak and chips for supper with apple pie for afters.

"The girls are delighted," Miss Kitty said, smiling at me, "I do like your young man, he will make you a good husband!"

"Not so fast, Miss Kitty, I have not got to that stage yet!"

"Well don't leave it too long or someone else will snap him up. He is a rare breed – a lovely man, just don't let him slip through your fingers!"

Nancy dropped a bombshell yesterday – we were all taken by surprise. She announced to us all that she is getting married to her boyfriend Ernie by special licence at the Registry Office next week!!! She has asked me if Bill and I would be witnesses.

I think the reason it is so sudden is because Ernie is being posted to Korea.

When we told Miss Kitty she said, "For goodness sake, what's the hurry – she has only known him for two months!"

Diana said, "So what, I expect they are madly in love!"

"Poppycock!" Miss Kitty retorted, "Mark my words, marry in haste repent at leisure!"

Marge, Joan and I took Nancy into Torquay to help her choose her outfit for the wedding which is in two days' time at the Registry Office in Newton Abbot. Nancy told us that the reason for the hurry was that Ernie was being posted, first to Catterick camp, up north, and then in two months' time to Korea. Ernie had given her enough money to buy what she needed and it was lovely to see Nancy happy and smiling as she had been looking so sad of late. She chose a silver grey suit with a black velvet collar and a frilly white blouse. Marge, Joan and I clubbed together to buy her a handbag to match and a pair of pretty white lace gloves. Well now, what about shoes? we asked,

"Oh, I'll wear these, they'll be alright!" We all looked down at her heavy, thick, brown brogue shoes and heavyweight stockings and said, "No you will not and not the stockings either." Marge exclaimed, "You, my lady, are going to have the finest silk stockings and dainty shoes we can find. So there!"

"But, I may not have enough money left," Nancy wailed.

"Don't you worry about that, we will all chip in and between us I'm sure we'll be able to buy you your shoes."

Under those ugly shoes, Nancy had the daintiest of feet and we all had a whale of a time choosing shoes for her. She decided on a pair of black patent court shoes and was thrilled with them. She walked up and down in the shoe shop, every so often glancing in the mirror and smiling to herself!

Mission accomplished, we then went on to Bobbies, on the seafront, for lunch. Nancy was still worrying about the money, and in the restaurant her attention was drawn to the cost of the meat!

"Nancy," Joan said, "It's a treat from Miss Kitty, so enjoy it!"

"But I'm overwhelmed by it all," she said, "I've never been in a place like this before!"

"This is the start of something good," I said, "and in two days' time you are to be married."

"Yes, to think I am going to be wed, I just can't believe all this is happening to me!" she replied.

Dear Nancy, bless her! I was thrilled to see her so happy. Miss Kitty's gift of money stretched to enable Nancy to buy a pair of cufflinks as a present for Ernie. What a lovely day we all had!

This morning we all helped Nancy with the fires. Diana was chief stoker and did a grand job, and Marge and I were the coal shovellers. 'Woe is me' Vera passed a sarcastic remark whilst passing through the kitchen, saying, "Well, I've seen it all now, are you two getting ready for your day of reckoning!"

"You cheeky madam!" shouted Margie, throwing a lump of coal in her direction. It missed but nearly hit a young recruit who was passing by. He joked, "All you girls needed to do was ask me to help!"

I replied, "We are so sorry, it was not intended for you."

"Well, Joe is here to help you lift those heavy buckets. You lovely young girls should not be doing that dirty job!" he said.

"For your gallantry," Marge replied, "come up to the kitchen for a coffee and a bun."

He grinned from ear to ear and said, "I like the idea of that, show me the way, young ladies." He picked up the two heavy buckets and Marge said to him, "You are one strong young man!" He winked at her and said, "At your service! Perhaps, if I am allowed, I will pass this way again!"

Diana whispered to me, "Where did he come from?" raising her eyes.

"From the coal!" I whispered back.

"Oh yeh! I ain't daft you know!" was her reply.

"Oh come on, Diana! Look after Joe, make him a coffee, in fact I will help you. We will all sit down and have a cup of coffee and a bun – we deserve it!"

'Woe is me' piped up, "Does Miss Kitty know about this set-up?"

Diana said to her, "Shut your cake hole or else…" giving her a menacing look and wielding the poker with which she had just been poking the fires.

"I was only checking!" stammered Vera.

"Oh yeh, you could have fooled me," retorted Diana.

We looked a real motley crew in our get-up, all wearing red and white check tea towels round our heads, and soot all over our faces! I am sure Diana had more soot on her than went into the bin!

Joe joked, "You all look great – why don't you all join the Army. You wouldn't look out of place on manoeuvres!"

"No thanks, this is only temporary," we replied.

When Joe took his leave of us he said, "If possible, I will be reporting for coal bucket duty tomorrow morning!"

"Please don't take any chances, Joe. It's very kind of you but it may get you into trouble. So we will all see you when you come into the canteen," I said. For one thing, I didn't really trust 'woe is me' Vera!

This afternoon Bill was off duty so we went into Newton Abbot to the cinema. These days I am on cloud nine. I am in love and I feel sure I have at last, found my Mr Right. Every day he writes me little love letters. I have truly never felt like this before. Oh yes, I have been in love before but, I can't explain how I feel, that he is *right* for me. It is this comfortable feeling I have when I am with him. Not like Robert who always made me feel on edge, as I knew I could never rely on him. He was always flitting off somewhere to the unknown *and* he was engaged. Then there was Mark, handsome and a lovely fellow, always the perfect gent. We shared interests in art and theatre but alas, he came with all these hang-ups. And then there were all the times he went AWOL and on drinking binges, so I was always unsure of him on that score. But then he had been to hell and back during the war and had to live with his demons. But Bill is such a funny guy, he makes me laugh and has a wonderful sense of humour. He is so kind and caring and I know in my heart that we will spend many happy years together. So, as the song goes, 'Love is a many splendored thing', it lifts your heart and all around you is transformed into a better place!

When we were cashing-up for the day, in the office last night Miss Kitty said, "What did I tell you, Eve," beaming at me.

"What?" I asked.

"Oh come on, you know, Bill, of course. He is the one for you, I'm right aren't I?"

"Yes," I replied.

Clapping her hands together, "I knew it, I knew it! Get that bottle of gin out of the cupboard behind you and let's make a toast," she said excitedly. In the next breath she asked, "When's the big day?" smiling at me.

"Well, he did propose but I said I would think about it."

"Think, think about it? What's wrong with you, girl? You love him, don't you?"

"Yes I do and he said he loves me deeply," I replied.

"Well what are you waiting for, girl?"

"Well, it's like this," I said, lamely, "it's all so sudden!"

"So sudden! What the hell are you waiting for, girl? Is he meeting you later?" she asked.

"No, he's on duty, Miss Kitty, but I will see him tomorrow when we go into Newton Abbot with Nancy to their wedding."

"Well, you jolly well say 'yes' to him then, do you hear me?"

"Yes, I do, Miss Kitty, goodnight. I'll see how the land lies tomorrow!" I replied.

"I despair!" she called after me.

Nancy and Ernie's wedding day and she was up with the lark and there was frantic activity in the billet. Marge helped Nancy to dress and I heated up the tongs for her hair. Miss Kitty had given her a pretty little pearl brooch with two intertwined hearts, for her suit jacket.

Bill had a friend who owned the Crown pub in Newton Abbot and who had a saloon car that he was able to borrow. So, we travelled in style to the registry office in a lovely car which purred along. Nancy was very quiet on the journey.

"What's wrong, Nancy?" Joan asked.

"I feel very queasy," she replied.

Bill said, "Don't worry, Nancy, you've just got pre-wedding collywobbles – you'll be alright!"

"I hope so," she said, wanly.

"She looks very pale," said Joan.

"Oh hell," said Bill, "has anybody got a paper bag? We don't want her throwing up in this car. My mate will have my guts for garters – this is his pride and joy!"

By a stroke of luck, Joan produced a large paper bag from her handbag and gave it to Nancy, "Now, hang on to that, Nancy, until we get there," and we all heaved a sigh of relief. It was just as well we weren't in the Army bus, the 'old bone-rattler'!

I never realised how austere a Registry office was and found it very impersonal. I also wondered where Nancy's family were as no one was present. However, Ernie and Nancy looked wonderful and so much in love when they were pronounced husband and wife. Afterwards we all went along to a local restaurant to have a late lunch and toast them both on their marriage. They were going to Torquay for a short honeymoon. Ernie had booked them into a hotel on the front for three days and Nancy looked so happy. He said that he planned to take Nancy to meet his parents on his next leave.

Back at the NAAFI it seemed very strange without little Nancy. Needless to say we are all on fire patrol and it is my turn tomorrow morning, with Diana.

I hope I will be able to drag her out of bed at 6.30 in the morning, as Marge said that Diana is going out on the town tonight with Roger – help!

Last night she rolled, or should I say fell in through the window at 1.30 and had a high old time trying to get into bed. Swearing, she said, "The bloody thing keeps moving, one of you lot come and help me!"

"Good morning, Diana," we chorused sleepily.

"Just lie on the bloody floor!" Margie shouted. The next thing we heard was an almighty thump and before long she was snoring away!

This morning I went over to Diana to wake her for our stint on lighting the fires, "Clear off," she slurred, "I ain't doing any fires!"

I had just about finished cleaning out the flues when she came staggering in to the kitchen looking much the worse for wear.

"My god, you look awful, what on earth were you drinking last night?" I asked.

"I don't know, I can't remember!" she said.

"What a state to get into!" I remarked.

"Shut up," she retorted, "my head is giving me gyp and I don't want you going on at me or I'll bail out and go back to bed."

"Well then, misery," I replied, "get hold of this pan of soot and go and empty it in the bin and I will go and make you and me a mug of coffee. Deal?" She muttered something rude so I added, "Mind how you go down the steps with that soot. We don't want you to land headlong into it!"

"Ha bloody ha!" she shouted back, "Put the bloody kettle on, big head!" She was in a hell of a strop! When she came back she said, "Eve, you honestly don't know how close you came to having that soot tipped over you!" I just smiled.

This afternoon, Margie and I are going into Newton Abbot to see if there is any more modelling on the horizon. We both agreed that our savings were looking a bit thin and needed a boost, but to our dismay we were told at the store that there was nothing at present but to try again next week.

I have a date with Bill tomorrow, which is my day off and we are going into Torquay. He is going to pack us up a picnic.

"Are you sure?" I asked him, "I could do that."

"No, my love, I have got it all set up. All I want you to do is ask the cooks for some Eccles cakes."

Picnic on the beach – I can't wait!

This morning, Diana woke me at 6.30, "What the hell are you doing up at this time in the morning? For heaven's sake go back to bed."

"Well, if you must know," she replied, "I've been awake most of the night with toothache, so I went to the kitchen and made a cup of tea and I thought I would do my good deed for the day and bring you one over."

"Thanks very much," I mumbled, "but have you forgotten it's my day off?"

"Well, I didn't know, you never tell me anything these days. And, by the way, misery guts, my tooth really is painful!"

"Go and take some aspirin and let me go back to sleep," I said, and she stormed out, banging the door on her way out which shook the room. There is something very much wrong with Diana, she seems very troubled these days.

I have left the best 'til last, I AM ENGAGED! Bill proposed to me, on the beach, on one knee, kneeling in the sand! It was so funny! He said, "My darling Eve, I love you deeply. For god's sake hurry up and say 'yes', my knee is killing me – I think I am kneeling on a blasted rock!" When we moved the sand away we found it was a broken bottle!

"Say 'yes' to what Bill?" I asked laughing.

"To marry me, of course."

"Well, my love, I will think about it," I teased, "for two seconds, and my answer is YES, yes!!" and with that he hugged me to him. My ring is white and gold with three diamonds that sparkle in the sunlight!

When you hear the phrase, 'my heart is singing', well, that is what mine felt like at that precious moment in time on that Torquay beach. My lovely man, my soul mate, I had found him at last! Many journeys I had travelled to get to this joyous moment in time.

Today I told Miss Kitty the good news of my engagement. She was overjoyed. "Splendid, my dear girl, I told you so, you were just meant for each other and to tell you the truth I was scared you would let that lovely man slip through your fingers. Open that cupboard behind you and let's toast your and Bill's future happiness."

"Miss Kitty," I said, "there is only brandy in here and a tonic water."

"Well, we'll have that then," she replied.

"But, I'm on duty in ten minutes!"

"Sit down, my dear girl, let them wait a few seconds," she said, smiling.

"Only a small one for me," I said, "or I will be doing a cabaret."

"Well, that would be something to write home about!" she replied with a chuckle. "All these weddings and engagements, if it goes on like this we will be short-staffed," Miss Kitty said.

Bill and I at Dembury Camp

"Oh it will be quite a while before I move on," I replied, "Your turn next, Miss Kitty!"

"Not on your Nellie," she replied, "I won't be venturing down that path!"

"But, Henry?" I enquired.

She laughed, "You must be joking, Eve. There is no way I could live with him, he's too set in his ways – a bit of an old woman at times! But, he will do for the present, alright to go out with on the odd occasion, but that's all!"

"I'm so sorry," I replied, "I didn't mean to pry."

"That's alright, my dear girl," she said, "I lost my true love during the war and I have never met anyone since to fill his shoes. My James was the love of my life, my shining light!"

"Miss Kitty, how sad."

"Let's just say that it is better to have loved and lost than never to have loved at all," she said with a sigh.

Today the camp was buzzing with new recruits, so it was all guns blazing on the bar, especially my net bar. I think I must have sold hundreds of dusters, boot polishes and Blancos, not forgetting the ciggies and chocolate bars.

The young, fresh-faced recruits were also trying their luck with the chat-up line and Diana was in her element! Naughty Diana, fluttering her eyelashes at them, oh well, I expect it cheered up their day! When I mentioned this to Margie she said, "It's alright for you up there at the end of your bar on your own but I am having to cope with her flirting and messing about! If you want my frank opinion I have come to the conclusion that she is a pain in the neck!"

"But you must admit, Margi, she is quite a character," I replied. She just walked away, rolling her eyes at me.

Nancy is back as Ernie has been posted to Yorkshire, and she hopes to join him soon.

Today Ruby said to me, "I think I might change my mind about being posted to Germany. My gran told me I was crazy to even have thought about it. She said to me, 'Rube, there will be all those foreign people out there and let's face it, girl, you don't speak any German and I have heard they are a rum lot'."

"Well, Ruby," I replied, "it is entirely up to you but I think your dear gran is a bit behind the times, after all you will be in a NAAFI for our troops and they all speak English."

"Do they really?" she asked.

"Of course they do, Ruby," I replied, "Bite the bullet and go and have an adventure!"

"What do you mean, Eve, about the bullet?" she asked suspiciously.

"It's just a figure of speech, Ruby," I said, "My advice to you is to go and talk it over with Miss Kitty. She will put you right, but don't mention the bullet!"

"But Eve, it does sound dangerous," she said.

"Oh, for goodness sake, Ruby," I said, "Miss Kitty will explain it all to you."

Give me strength, I thought, how on earth has she managed all her tender years?!

"Good luck, Ruby," I said, "See you later, I have troops to serve on the bar."

Later Miss Kitty caught me and said, "What the hell did you send that stupid girl to me for? My god, she drove me round the bend! I had one hell of a time trying to explain the ins and outs of this posting. Personally, I don't think she is safe to go out there. It would be a good idea, Evie for you to talk her out of it and be careful how you word it this time. For goodness sake, cut out the adventure bit and the bullet bit! The poor girl doesn't get the gist of it at all, it's all foreign to her!"

They are very fond of passing the buck around here! I shall have to learn to say 'no' more often, although being me, it's difficult.

Chapter 18

Just when I thought everything was going smoothly, yesterday morning Nancy gave me a hell of a shock. She woke me at ten to six saying, "Eve, wake up! Quickly, it's coming!"

Half dozy with sleep I said, "What's coming? Go back to bed. You've had a nightmare!"

"No, no, help me please! I am having a baby!"

I shot up in bed, "What, Nancy, did you say… BABY??!!!"

"Yes, yes, it's coming!" and there she was lying doubled up across the foot of my bed.

I dashed down the corridor to Miss Kitty's room, knocked on the door and put the light on as I walked in. She sat bolt upright in bed. Despite the seriousness of the situation this is what confronted me – there was Miss Kitty in her winceyette nightgown with frills around the neck, with a pair of frilly, pink knickers on her head from which protruded two dinky curlers standing up on each side of her head, looking like horns. Not unlike Widow Twanky from the pantomime! And on her bedside table were her teeth in a jam jar! If I had not found myself in such a dramatic situation I would have had the urge to laugh out loud!

"For god's sake, what's wrong Eve? Is the canteen on fire?"

"No, no Miss Kitty," I said, "it's Nancy. She's having a baby!"

"A baby, a baby! Are you out of your mind bursting in here at this time of the morning. It's bloody impossible, she's only been married six weeks! Tell her to get back in bed, it was one hell of a nightmare she's had. Stupid girl!"

"No, no, it's not that. She *is* having a baby," I pleaded, "she needs help and is at present lying on my bed doubled up in pain and says that her waters have broken! Also she's peed herself and it's all over the floor. What shall I do? Shall I send for the medical officer on camp?"

"No, no certainly not!" she answered angrily, "Get her off the camp, she is not having no baby here, do you hear me, Eve, not in my NAAFI!!"

In despair at her attitude I was at a loss at what she expected me to do. In fact I was more worried about poor Nancy about to give birth on my bed, so angrily I answered her, "You have to do something for the poor girl, now!"

"Well, well, calm down, let's think," she said. Then, "I've had an idea. You, my dear girl, go and ask Bill to help. He can take my Austin, he does drive?"

"Yes," I replied.

"Well, that's splendid! You can go with him and take her into Newton Abbot to the hospital there."

"But I can't go and get Bill. I don't even know where his billet is," I pleaded with her.

"Well, Eve, I can't go. I have to stay here and keep everything afloat and you are much calmer than me and cope better when situations arise, you have that gift!" she blustered.

I had no answer to that although there was quite a lot I wanted to say, going something along the line of, 'to hell with all that flannel of having a gift, who are you kidding, you just do not want to put yourself out!'

So, here I go again, being nursie and if I don't get a move on, a midwife as well. I gave Miss Kitty's door a good bang on my way out and in the corridor bumped into Joan. She said, "Don't worry, Evie, I will keep an eye on Nancy while you go over and find Bill."

"But Joan, that's the problem, I don't know where his billet is. As you know, it's like a vast maze on this camp and it is dark!"

"Well," Joan replied, "go and knock on the cookhouse door, there is bound to be someone there I expect, getting the troops' breakfasts ready at this time."

I quickly got dressed and put a brush through my hair and made my way over to the cookhouse.

I banged loudly on the massive doors to the cookhouse. Lofty, the cook opened the doors and asked, "What's wrong, Eve?"

"Please, Lofty, will you go and get Bill. It is urgent!" He beckoned for me to go in. There was a sight to behold! Frank Vincent, who was a dwarf and a mascot in the regiment, was standing on a wooden platform, stirring porridge in a great cooking pot. Lofty said to him, "Go over, Titch, and get Bill to come over here pronto. Tell him Eve wants him urgently."

Frank stamped his little feet and said to Lofty, "You bloody well go, not me!" With that, Lofty picked him up by the scruff of the neck and dangled him over the cauldron of steaming hot porridge. His little legs were going like pistons!

"For goodness sake, Lofty," I said, "put him down and stop messing about. This is a very urgent mission I'm on, so please, one of you, please, please go and get Bill." There was Nancy about to give birth, I thought, and these two idiots are mucking about!

"Oh hell, I'll go, I have the longest legs," Lofty said, "You go back to the NAAFI and I will send Bill over. Eve, don't worry, I'm sure everything will be alright!"

"I hope so too, Lofty. More than you know!" I replied.

Joan had sorted Nancy out with her bag ready for the hospital. I noticed that there were baby clothes in there and napkins – she must have known all along. I was cross but just went on to help her on her journey. Bill came over and was so relieved that I was alright, he thought I had had an accident.

Lofty had scared the daylights out of him and told him to get over to me as something terrible had happened.

"Well, what's wrong then, Evie?" he asked me.

"It's Nancy, she's having a baby!"

"What baby? Well, what has that got to do with me?"

"Well, my love, you are taking us to the hospital in Newton Abbot!"

"NO. No way, Eve, no way! I have no transport."

"Miss Kitty said you could drive her Austin 7."

"Oh, did she now," he replied.

Joan said to him, "Please Bill, do help us, she's in labour!"

"Oh, alright then, let's get the old jalopy cranked up. Who's coming along with me beside Eve and Nancy?"

"I'm coming too," said Joan, "I'll sit in the back with her."

"Right, pile in quick. Let's get her there quickly!"

The old car's exhaust spit and sputtered and we raced through those camp gates with bangs and creaks in a trail of smoke. The guard on the gate looked at us with open-mouthed amazement when we shot through the gates surrounded by smoke.

"Bloody hell, this old banger is juddering and creaking so much we'd better all pray it doesn't break down before we get

Nancy to the hospital," said Bill. "Nancy, be prepared, you may end up being delivered in one of those farm barns on the way!"

"Who is going to be the midwife?" Joan asked.

"Count me out," said Bill.

"Me too!" I said weakly.

"Thanks, you lot," said Joan, "that only leaves me and I only came along for the ride!"

It was just as well that it was early morning and there was not much traffic on the road. Bill asked me, when did Miss Kitty put any petrol in this jalopy and I said that I didn't know.

"Did you not think to ask?" said Bill.

"Well no, there was too much going on to ask or even think about it."

"Well," he said, "cars don't run on water, you know!"

"There's no need to be sarcastic," I said, "Which side of the bed did you get out of this morning?"

"Well, my love, I was hustled out of my warm bed to help a damsel in distress, at your command! The gauge doesn't indicate anything so I expect it's OK, but let's pray anyhow!"

We, at last, managed to chug our way into the centre of the town. There was a policeman on the roundabout directing traffic. Bill asked Nancy if was left or right to the hospital and she said she didn't know.

"Oh well, I'll stop and ask the Bobbie." He wound down the window and the policeman came over and asked, "Are you lost, mate?"

"Well, yes in a way. We would like directions to the hospital."

"Just take the right turn and it's up the hill on the left-hand side. Good luck, mate," he said.

We pulled up outside the hospital and I got out and knocked on this massive door which echoed inside. A starched Matron opened the door and asked very curtly, "How can I help you?"

I replied, "We have a young lady in the car and she is in labour and it is very advanced!"

"Well, it is no use you coming here, you want the Maternity hospital!" and with a toss of her starched head, she closed the doors with a bang.

When I returned to the car Bill asked, "Shall I get Nancy out?"

"No, wrong hospital! We have to go to the Maternity one!"

"Did you ask her where it is?"

"Well no, she didn't give me a chance. She was so cross with me for not knowing!"

"Well, back down the road and round the roundabout, I suppose," he said, with a sigh.

The policeman was surprised to see us again so soon, "Well mate, did you not find it?"

"Wrong hospital!" said Bill,

The policeman put his head through the window and looked at us all and said, smiling at Bill, "Congratulations, mate!"

"Not me, not me! I ain't got nothing to do with it, I'm just the driver," Bill protested, looking all flustered.

The policeman laughed and rolled his eyes and said, "Left turn then up the hill and it's on the right near the pub. Good luck, anyhow, hope you get there in time!"

We pulled up outside the Maternity hospital and I got out and knocked once again on another closed door. As I waited outside I said a little prayer, 'Please, please God, let someone answer'.

Eventually, the door opened and a sister asked me, "Can I help you, dear?"

"Yes, yes you can! But it's not for me, we've got a young lady in the back of the car and she's in strong labour."

"Well, of course," she said, "is she registered?"

"Yes, yes," I said, not knowing whether she was or not. But I just wanted her quickly out of that car into safe hands.

"First of all, my dear, go and ask her whether it's her first or second baby."

"Oh, it's her first," I said.

"Go and ask anyway," said the nurse.

I ran over to the car to ask Nancy, and asked her quietly, "Nancy, is it your first or second baby? Please don't be offended at me asking but they want to know."

"Third!" she replied. To say I was in shock was an understatement!

I ran back over and told the sister and she replied, "Better get her in here quick!"

Joan and I helped her out of the back seat. She was in a sorry state, doubled up in agony. On seeing our distress, the kind sister went back in and sent out a nurse with a wheelchair for Nancy. When she was safely wheeled away to the labour ward, we asked the sister for their phone number so that we could ring later to find out how she was.

"Don't worry, we will take care of her and the baby. Come and visit tomorrow."

"Many thanks to you, Sister," I said.

"We don't need thanks," she said, "that's what we're here for, my dear. Good luck on your journey back to camp and see you tomorrow."

Once we were all back in the car, I slumped back exhausted and said, "Thank god that's over with! I don't know about you both, but I'm starving, let's go and get something to eat before we go back to camp."

"Now that is a jolly good idea, Evie," said Bill, "Let's hope the old jalopy will start up again."

But lo and behold, the old car had not got a spark of life in her. So Bill got out and gave her a good crank, saying a few swear words and threatening her with the scrapyard.

Joan and I laughed but Bill said, "Sorry, ladies, but you will both have to get out and give her a push down the hill. That should get it going."

That was when I spotted that Joan was still in her curlers which, to be honest I had not noticed with all the mayhem of Nancy. Looking down at my feet I saw that I still had on my furry, pink slippers.

"Joan," I said, "you still have your curlers in."

"So what," she laughed, "You're still wearing your slippers!"

We both curled up with mirth.

"Come on, you two," called Bill, "put your strength behind this rust bucket."

It was a good job we were going downhill, not up, as eventually, after much pushing and puffing, the old girl spluttered into life with a loud bang and clouds of exhaust fumes. We fell into the moving car.

"Bill," I said, "Why didn't you tell me I was wearing my slippers?"

"I didn't notice, anyway so what," he chuckled, "you look lovely anyhow, pink, furry slippers and all!"

We stopped at a small café for a late breakfast. On entering, Joan and I made a beeline for a secluded table in the corner. I tucked my slippered feet under the table, out of sight and Joan had managed to remove some of her curlers but when Bill called out to come and see what we wanted to eat we both shouted out, "We'll have what you are having!"

When it arrived it was bacon, sausage, egg, black pudding (ugh), fried bread, tomato and to add to this plate of plenty, chips and toast.

Joan remarked, "If I eat all that I will need a kip when I get back to camp!"

Bill said, "Get it down you. It will set you up for the day and stick your ribs together."

The place soon started filling up with lorry drivers. It was obviously their place for meeting their mates and refuelling on these generous helpings of breakfast foods. But my dilemma was how to get out of there without any of them noticing my slippers. I managed to get as far as the door and then there was a loud chorus of wolf whistles and I was through that door like a bat out of hell!

Our luck held and the car started up first time and so we headed back to camp.

"Back to the rat-race!" Bill mused, "Eve, will you please let me know, in good time, if you have any more surprises for me on the horizon because this early morning stint does not agree with me!"

"I'll second that!" chirped up Joan, "It plays havoc with my beauty sleep!"

How could I answer that? All I could think of was that I had been in the wrong place at the wrong time! The story of my life! Ever the optimist, I looked across at Bill's cheery face and thought, it can only get better with such a lovely man like him at my side.

Chapter 19

On our return to camp, Joan and I were taken aback by Marge and 'woe is me' Vera who attacked us with, "You took your time!"

"Where the hell have you been? Making the most of the situation, I bet! You've been skiving off," accused Marge, aggressively.

"Oh, for goodness sake, Margi," I replied, "you have not got a clue about what sort of a morning we've had. So if you don't mind, Joan and I are now going into the office to report back to Miss Kitty. So, do please excuse me!"

On our way to the office Joan said, "Well, that certainly took the wind out of their sails!"

But I have my doubts about that. It was certainly a relief to be back but my thoughts were with my fiancé Bill, hoping that he would not get into trouble, although he did say that his mates would cover for him.

We were greeted by, "Well done, you both did a grand job!" from Miss Kitty, "Off you both go and take the rest of the day off."

I was just dozing off on my bed when Marge burst into the room. She was still on her high horse, "Do you realise I had to take over the net bar while you were away and I was run off my feet and had an endless queue and to top it all they were all asking where you were!" she ended sarcastically.

"Oh, go away Margi, my advice to you is to go and see Miss Kitty. She will fill you in on the situation you seem to find yourself in. Oh, and Margi, sarcasm is the lowest form of wit, so stick that in your pipe and smoke it! Oh, and shut the door on your way out, Miss high and mighty." I just did not have the energy left for a spat with her.

I was woken later by Diana who came in saying, "Come on sleeping beauty, wake up, I have brought you tea and cake."

"What time is it?" I asked.

"Four fifteen, you have slept for three hours."

"Oh, I must get up."

"Now you just stay where you are, Miss Kitty's orders," Diana replied. "It's my day off and later on you and I are going to the farm. Roger's parents have invited us to supper. Bill came in earlier to see how you are and I told him you were sleeping, and by the way, he is invited too so we will be a foursome. Roger is picking us up at seven, so you have plenty of time to get ready," she said and plonked herself down on my bed. She grabbed a blanket from the foot of Nancy's bed and wrapped it round her, just like a squaw.

"It's blasted cold in this joint," she said, laughing, "When we've had our tea I'll stoke up that metal monster. By the way, that Marge is going around the canteen with a face as long as a fiddler's elbow! Whatever have you done to her, Eve, she ain't no fun anymore?"

"Nothing," I replied.

"'Woe is me' Vera is woe-meing and saying we are all crazy and she is going to leave. I said goodbye to her and asked if she'd like some help with her packing. She was cutting up onions at the time and she threw one at me but I ducked and it hit Henry right in the 'bread basket'! It was so funny, Eve, he walked through the door at that precise minute. He mumbled, all red in the face, 'Can anyone play?' Vera's face was a picture! Oh, Eve, it was hilarious!"

Thank goodness, I thought, we have the funny old Diana back to liven us all up. It was a tonic after the day I had had.

Joan came in, hearing all the laughter, "I just had to come and join you," she said. Diana related to her the run-in with Vera and then Joan turned to me and said, "Eve, I can't help thinking about you and your pink slippers and you were totally unaware of wearing them and me in my dinky curlers and every time I think about it I giggle to myself… and dear Bill, he took it all in his stride, bless him!"

"It will be something I will remember for a very long time, that's for sure," I replied, "Also, the startled look on Miss Kitty's face when I told her that Nancy was about to give birth and not forgetting little Frank being held over the pot of porridge with his little legs going hell for leather like pistons!"

By this time we were all helpless with laughter.

"No wonder the traffic cop was grinning from ear to ear and rolling his eyes when he put his head into the car and looked us all over! And Bill saying, it's not mine, I have nothing to do with it, I'm only the driver!"

Diana asked, "Why didn't you wake me? I would have come with you."

"Well, if you remember, Diana, you told me to sod off!" I replied.

"Oh, did I say that?" all innocent.

"Yes, you did," retorted Joan. "But, in any case it would have been a dilemma where to put you in the old jalopy."

"Well, Evie, I could have come instead of Joan," she replied.

"It's just as well you didn't," replied Joan, "as I wouldn't have missed it for the world and it certainly beats making cakes and putting up with 'woe is me' Vera giving me earache!"

This morning, everything was back to normal apart from Marge, who now was not speaking to me. It is so childish and it baffles me at what she is so peeved about.

Hospital news – Nancy was delivered of a bouncing baby boy weighing in at 9lbs 4oz. He was born ten minutes after we left. It amazes me how she kept her pregnancy so well hidden and to think she had been lifting those heavy buckets of coal, day in and day out.

Joan said, "To think, Eve, it could have been born on the back seat of that old car or any time!"

"Oh don't," I replied, "it gives me the heebie-jeebies just thinking about it!"

This afternoon we went into town to visit Nancy. Joan had been round collecting donations towards a present for Nancy and the baby and she and Diana came to the hospital. They had asked Marge to come too but she had declined saying she had better things to do with her precious time off.

So, no change there then!

When we were cashing-up in the office at lunch time Miss Kitty said to me, "I really am so sorry that you had to carry the can for me but I had to be here in case the district manager turned up. Also, I knew that you would cope with it better than me, and you had Joan's help. I had every faith in your ability to cope well in a crisis and mark my words, you are going to make a good manageress."

On looking over at her, I still had the vision in my head of the frilly knickers on her head and the two dinky curlers sticking out like horns and it was as much as I could do to stifle a giggle before answering, "Thank you, Miss Kitty, for your vote of confidence in me."

"What's so funny, Eve?" she asked, looking puzzled.

"Nothing at all, I was just thinking about me and my pink slippers!"

Thinking to myself, they would have made a good match with the pink frilly knickers! Oh, what a day that was, I couldn't get out of there fast enough!

All that must be kept a well-guarded secret as gossip goes round like wildfire here. I do have a soft spot for Miss Kitty. I know she can be a bit prickly at times but there is no doubt that she is a good egg. Although, I did go right off her yesterday when she landed me and Bill in it, but let's hope nothing like that arises again!

Nancy was looking quite radiant, sitting up in bed but when I remarked on how well she was looking she replied, "Looks are deceiving, Eve, I'm worried sick about what Ernie will say when he knows it's not his baby!"

"Well, don't worry too much about it now. Get yourself well and perhaps when he sees the lovely little baby boy, his heart will melt," I tried.

"I doubt it very much, Eve. I told him it was his child and that is why we married so quickly!"

"Oh Nancy, I don't know what to say," I replied, "Just look on the bright side for now. If Ernie loves you I'm sure he will forgive you."

"Please don't tell him about the other two, will you? If he does come back to the camp please don't tell him, promise?!!"

"My answer to that, Nancy, is that my lips are sealed. That is entirely your business and not for anyone else to divulge. We will come to see you again in two days, so take care of yourself 'til then."

Out of earshot, Joan said to me, "What a mess! Poor girl, I do hope Ernie forgives her."

Diana said, "Let's hope!"

I sighed.

Tomorrow morning I have another task to perform. Miss Kitty has asked me to look after Ernie who is coming to the camp and then to the NAAFI and has asked to speak to me concerning Nancy's sudden departure to hospital and the baby, before he goes on to the hospital to visit them both. I have performed many roles since being here but this one I am not looking forward to at all. I asked Miss Kitty if she would be there too at this meeting, but her reply was, "I'm afraid not. I have an appointment with the district manager. Sorry, Eve."

Oh yeah, I thought, very convenient! Perhaps I should change my job to 'Welfare'. Alas, Joan was on leave, so it looks like I have to go it alone.

"Don't look so worried, my dear," said Miss Kitty, smiling, "You were wonderful the other day, getting Nancy to hospital. This will only be filling him in on the circumstances of the poor girl!"

It is exactly that, that scares the hell out of me, I thought.

Ernie arrived at the unearthly hour of seven in the morning. Everyone in the billet was snoring their heads off and it was just as well I was up and dressed. After having had a restless night I had risen early and there he was, banging loudly on the billet door as though his life depended on it.

"There is no need to bang so loud, there are people asleep in here," I said to him.

"Well, I've been out of my mind with worry," he replied, "and unable to sleep."

Me too, mate, I thought, and this mess is nothing to do with me either, I just got railroaded into it. I took him up to the kitchen in the canteen.

"First of all, I would like you to sit down, Ernie, and I will make you a cup of coffee," I said, as I could see that he was all pent-up with anger and ready to explode. After a while he seemed to calm down but when he asked me if the baby was premature, I answered, "No, Ernie. He weighed in at nine pounds four ounces."

He slammed his mug of coffee down with such a force that it sprayed all over the table and ran in rivulets on to the floor. He stormed round the kitchen like a caged animal shouting at me, "You are a bloody liar!"

By now I was really scared and at my wits' end not knowing how to deal with him.

"Ernie," I called out to him, "For goodness sake sit down and let me try to explain everything to you. Because if you don't I am going to have to call for help here."

He sat down again, at the table.

"Ernie, you are scaring me," I said, "I am only trying to help you and after all I didn't have to agree to meet you, so please listen."

He sat with his head in his hands.

"Please Ernie," I said as calmly as I could, although my voice was shaky, "Go and see Nancy and let her tell you everything. I cannot tell you any more."

He got up from his chair like a broken man with tears streaming down his face and walked toward the door.

"Good bye, Ernie, give my love to Nancy," I said and he turned to me sobbing and said, "Whatever is my mother going to say?" I had no answer to that.

On closing the door I went back into the kitchen and poured myself a strong cup of coffee, wishing that I had a brandy to accompany it. I felt as though I had been on a roller coaster of events from which I had no escape!

Later on, when cashing-up, Miss Kitty looked over at me saying, "You don't look very well. Go back to the billet and rest. Take the rest of the day off – and tomorrow."

"But, what about the net bar?" I asked.

"Let me worry about that, now off you go. You have earned this time off!"

I did not need telling twice. I was just about at the end of my tether!

I flaked out on my bed and slept.

I was woken by Diana saying, "Wakey, wakey, sleeping beauty! Prince Charming is awaiting your presence in the kitchen and looking so handsome!"

"Who?" I asked, sleepily.

"Who else are you expecting, Evie? It's that handsome man called Bill – your future husband! I have brought you over a mug of tea and some Eccles cakes, your favourites, compliments of the cook of the day, 'woe is me' Vera!"

Now, there's a surprise! The old girl has got a heart, after all!

"So, get that down you and put on your finery," continued Diana, "Bill is dressed to kill! He has on a tweed jacket and brown corduroy trousers and his brown shoes are so shiny, polished that you can see your face in them! He looks so smart, a real gent!"

"So, why is he in civvies?" I asked.

"That is for you to find out!" she laughed.

I put on my new navy suit, with the jacket nipped in at the waist and navy pleated skirt. My blouse was white with a red stripe and to complete the ensemble, I put on my red court shoes. I really felt that I wanted to dress up after the morning I had had with Ernie.

Bill was waiting for me on the steps of the billet. He greeted me with, "You look a picture! Come on, lovely lady, we're going for a spin. I have been loaned a car from my mate Bob, who owns the pub in Newton Abbot. So, if it's alright with you, we can get away from this place for a while and stay overnight in Torquay. So, in you go and pack a bag for overnight – I assume that is a 'Yes'!" he finished, smiling.

"Yes, yes! But I will have to let Miss Kitty know."

"No need, I have already fixed it! After all, I'm not called Mr Fixit for nothing," he chuckled.

The car was a shiny, black Wolsey and it purred along on the way to Newton Abbot.

"Where are we going, Bill?" I asked.

"It's a mystery tour, just sit back and enjoy the scenery."

"But, you said Torquay…"

"Yes, we will end up there later but in the meantime we are going to a lovely little village. So relax, my love, we are away from that place so let's enjoy this time together."

"How long have you known your mate Bob?" I asked.

"Questions, questions!" he replied, "I'll just say that he is a good mate. Now it's just you and me time, so let's both enjoy this time away from the camp because I want to have time to talk things over with you concerning our forthcoming wedding."

We pulled up in a lovely village called Cockington. It was so picturesque, in beautiful grounds set with rhododendrons in full bloom. The colours were quite magnificent – reds, pinks, purples, blues and greens – it was quite a setting. There was a blacksmith with a real anvil and a small gift shop which sold, among other things, lucky silver horseshoes and little pixies called 'Joan of the Wad' that were also supposed to bring luck. Bill bought me a 'Joan of the Wad' to put in my purse and a silver horseshoe to, "Bring you all the luck in the world, my love," he said.

"Shall I buy you one then, Bill?" I asked him.

"I don't need anything like that," he replied, smiling at me, "My luck is you! What more do I want, knowing that you are by my side!"

It amazed me how many people Bill knew! For instance, when we eventually got to Torquay we stayed in a small hotel at which, the owners, Jack and Linda, welcomed him with open arms.

"My, you are very popular!" I said.

"Oh, I just do the odd job for them like plucking and dressing pheasants and the odd chicken or turkey when they have a party on. Of course," he said, winking at me and with that devilish twinkle in his eye, "only when I'm not on duty!"

We were invited to stay for lunch the next day. Linda was a tiny lady, full of bounce and she buzzed around the place like a busy bee. Jack was a more serious type, more laid back and he said to us, "Lindy wears me out! I honestly don't know where she gets her energy from."

"It's all that sea air and good living," Bill said.

"If you say so!" Jack replied, mopping his forehead and rolling his eyes.

On leaving, they hugged us both saying, "Now don't forget, think about having your wedding in Torquay. For a grand couple like you we would put on a wonderful spread!"

Chapter 20

Back at camp this morning, Marge was in one of her foul moods so I just had to tackle her about what was wrong. At first she was quite hostile but I persevered and said, "Now, Marge, do tell me. Is it something I have done wrong by you?" although I could not for the life of me, think what!

"No, no not really," she replied, "But now you have Bill and are planning to marry, I am of no use to you any more!"

"Oh, come on, Marge, my marrying Bill would not possibly come between our friendship."

"You say that!" she retorted defiantly, "Oh, and another thing…" There was a long pause from her.

"Well, what is it?" I asked.

She uttered quietly, as if it were too painful for her to put into words, "Everyone likes you and you get carried along with it and exclude me. Miss Kitty asks you, not me, to do things!"

"Well, Marge," I answered, "I'll tell you what, you would be more than welcome to take on some of the jobs I am asked to do! Shall I put your name forward?"

"Oh no, don't do that!"

"Well then, there we are, all this aggro for nothing!"

Then she blurted out, "Vera told me it was not fair!"

Ha! I thought, that is where this is all coming from!

"Forget Vera or should I say, 'Woe is me'! Are we friends again?" I asked.

"Yes, alright then, Evie, but you will include me into things won't you?"

"I certainly will," I replied, "Now, are you sure I can't put in a good word with Miss Kitty for some of those tasks for you?" I said, teasing her. She frowned at me, "Don't you dare!"

That old saying, 'you never know anyone until you live with them' is so true. That close friendship with Marge will never be the same. Perhaps it's just as well that my time here is coming to an end. Bill and I have set a date for our forthcoming wedding for December 18th and that is in only three and a half months' time. We have decided to get married in Bill's home town, in the church there, in Watlington, Oxfordshire. I have heard so much about this beautiful, small town and we are going there to meet Bill's family on my next long weekend off, which is coming up shortly.

Today Marge, Diana and I went to visit Nancy but alas, when we got there Nancy and the baby had left. The sister in charge told us that after the visit from her husband she had left the next day. But, where did she go? we asked. The sister didn't know, she just told us that Nancy had left on her own with the baby. We did a painstaking search of known haunts, to no avail. It was hopeless, she just seemed to have vanished. In my heart I hoped that Ernie had forgiven her, I so wanted a happy ending for Nancy and her baby boy.

This morning, Marge told me that she and Lance were back together and have decided to marry next year. I told her that it was lovely news and to let me know when their big day was to be.

Next weekend I am going to Watlington to meet Bill's parents and family. He has told me that the townspeople are very friendly and they make you feel so welcome, like belonging to one large family. It sounds so much nicer than living in a large town which can be very cold and lonely. Bill summed it up, "There is so much warmth from everyone, so for me, it beats large towns hands down."

I loved hearing Bill's stories about his home town. He worked as a butcher in the High Street and also a part-time fireman before being called up for National Service. The family home was originally in Greenwich, where Bill was born, until they were bombed out during the Blitz. They lost their home and the family, Mum, Dad, Bill, brother and sisters were evacuated to Ewelme, a village not far from Watlington. A local farmer, very kindly offered them a home in his farmhouse and told them that they were welcome to stay until they got back on their feet. It would also give them breathing space while they looked around for somewhere to rent. Bill's mum offered to do the housekeeping for him, as he told them that he had not long lost his wife, and his dad managed to get employment at the nearby RAF Station at Benson. Eleven-year-old Bill was enrolled at Ewelme School and he also volunteered to look after the chickens for the farmer, collecting the eggs and feeding them before school. Then, he said, he also helped by chopping logs for the fires and did a paper round in the village and then later on, helped with his teacher's vegetable garden. It was 'all hands on deck', but then that is what it was like during the War, everyone pulled together. Eventually, they had the luck to rent a large flat in Watlington and Bill and his siblings transferred to the school there.

He also told me a story about an amazing coincidence that happened to him when he was on a posting in Singapore. Bill said that he was walking past the famous Raffles Hotel, thinking, 'I wish I could just go in there, walk to the bar and order a drink.' Then, striding towards him was General Sir John Mogg, a man he knew well from Watlington, as he, his wife Lady Margaret and his family were regular customers at the butcher's shop where Bill worked.

"Well, well, what are you doing here, so far from home, Butcher Bill?" the General said, "It's so good to see you! Come, let's go celebrate our meeting up so far from home!"

"But, Sir, I won't be allowed in there. I'm only an NCO."

"Rubbish, Bill, come along, you are my guest!"

What a small world it is... And so, his wish was granted!

Bill and I arrived back at camp late last night. Everything went well in Watlington and Bill's parents welcomed me into the family and were delighted about our forthcoming wedding. We went along to the vicarage to meet Vicar Lewis and I found him a kind, charming man who was very friendly and helpful. We agreed on the date for our wedding, the 18th of December, even though it will be on a Wednesday. We had hoped for a Saturday, but as Vicar Lewis explained, 'it is Advent', and Christmas is always a busy time in church. What a lovely town! My heart was warmed by the number of people Bill introduced me to and they all seemed very kind and friendly. Perhaps, one day, Bill and I will settle down here when our Service days are over. I have moved around the countryside a lot, especially during the War, but never found anywhere as unique as Watlington, which nestles in a valley surrounded by the Chiltern Hills amid beautiful scenic countryside. It is a very special place and as Bill had said, the townspeople are like a big welcoming family.

Miss Kitty said to me this morning, "I'm so pleased you are back, Eve, we have been run off our feet. Your friend Marge is away in Birmingham on unexpected leave. Something to do with that boyfriend of hers, do you by any chance know what that is all about?"

"No, I'm afraid not, Miss Kitty, I am as puzzled as you," I replied.

Bill came into the canteen this morning and dropped one almighty bombshell. He is being posted to Egypt for two years, so the beginning of our married life will be very short. To think he will be so far away, why oh why could they not have given him a posting in this country? Or Germany, at least I would have been able to join him there. Next week he is being posted to Borden, near Aldershot, with the rest of his company so I have asked Miss Kitty if it would be possible for me to have a posting to the NAAFI in Borden. She said she would do her utmost for me, so I am keeping my fingers crossed.

Only ten days until my wedding and I am missing Bill already and he has only been gone two days! I can't bear the thought of him being away for two years in Port Said. We will only have four weeks together as man and wife and I honestly can't think, at the moment, how I am going to cope for those two years!

This morning, after having a heart-to-heart talk with Miss Kitty last night, I can honestly say that I am not feeling sorry for myself anymore. Miss Kitty gave me some good news of my posting to Borden and I will be leaving here at the weekend. She has arranged for me to go on leave until after Christmas and gave me another piece of good news, "For you, my dear, are going to St Lucia NAAFI at Borden as a trainee manageress! Those two years will fly by, Eve, and later on you may get a posting out there to be near him. So, things are not so bad then, so come on, my dear, let's see that lovely smile and promise me that you will come and stay from time to time!" she said, then added, wiping a tear from her eye, "I will miss you, my dear, but now run along and go and phone Bill with your good news."

Walking to the post box later on in the day, I bumped into Lofty and little Frank, the cooks. I still had that vision of little Frank being dangled over the porridge pot with his little legs going like pistons!

Lofty said to me, "You are coming to the cook house with us, now!"

"But, why? What for?" I asked.

"We have a surprise for you, Eve!" So, off we went to the cook house.

Jokingly, little Frank said, "Lofty sat me on his knee and we put our two heads together to make this for you both!"

And, lifting a white tablecloth, there was a beautifully decorated wedding cake! It was three tiers and on the top was a bride and groom and there were silver horseshoes and butterflies and I was overcome!

The two of them stood there, grinning from ear to ear, "Well, say something! Do you like it?" they asked eagerly.

I was so overcome to think they must have spent hours on it, I thought. "Yes, yes I love it! It is amazing, a work of art, you are so clever!" I replied.

What a lovely gift!

"When Bill and I return for a few days after our wedding, we will celebrate with you two dear friends!" I said.

"Give our best to Butch and tell him that we miss his steaks and his corny jokes! We have arranged for the cake to go by one of the transport lorries to Borden," said Lofty, "Oh, and ask Butch if he could wangle a posting for this little perisher," he said, laughing, "I'll buy him a bucket and spade!"

I left them with little Frank chasing Lofty around the room. What a comical pair they are, but lovely characters!

So, here ends another chapter of my life as a NAAFI girl, and another one to start at Borden. But, that is another story for another day.

About the Author

I spent the War years in the Women's Land Army. Then when the War ended I joined the NAAFI. It was around the time when the National Service came into being, when young men were called up to serve for two years either in the Army, Royal Air Force or Navy or other services. Many of these young recruits were very young and many leaving their homes for the first time. Those difficult times brought people together from all walks of life and in unexpected ways. Many tender friendships began and love blossomed. So this is my story about all those amazing characters that I met in the line of duty and which enriched my life.

I met Mrs Hastings (Sandy) at the Union Jack Club where I was kindly invited as a guest. At that time I was nearing the end of writing my manuscript of *Diary of a NAAFI Girl*. My memories of the time I spent in the NAAFI. On meeting the ex-NAAFI ladies I felt I just had to give them a mention in my book. So here are their stories:

Mrs Sandy Hastings

I served in the Middle East for two years. First I was in Egypt where I spent six months and got to see the pyramids and the sphinx, but alas, this came to an abrupt end and I was sent to Palestine where everything unfurled into chaos and danger.

There was a terrorist gang operating in the area at the time. They kidnapped two sergeants from our camp and then hanged them in the orange groves. Naturally there was a lot of unrest amongst the troops. The terrorists went on to blow up the King David Hotel in Jerusalem, killing many people. All in all it was not a very happy place at the time. However, it was a wonderful experience and I finished my two years in the NAAFI in Palestine. Although life was very uncertain due to the unrest, I sailed through it all. I even managed a visit to Bethlehem at Christmas time.

Mrs Patricia Sheldrick

I joined the ATS in 1944 and was posted to an army barracks in Dalkieth, and from there to Gypsy Hill NAAFI HQ. I was then posted to the accounts section of the NAAFI in the George Hotel in Edinburgh. After this I was posted to Ismailia in Egypt where I worked for two years in an office with Tommy Booth, who at the time was a sergeant, but later became a major. I returned to the UK on leave before returning to Egypt for a few months, before volunteering to go to Palestine for the close of the mandate. That was a journey into great unrest and terrorism, but eventually I was posted to Nairobi in Kenya where I was de-mobbed in 1949. All in all, and despite the chaos of the time, I enjoyed my time serving in the NAAFI.